Jayne Collier and her husband, Andrew, opened Axe Valley Bird and Animal Park to the public in 2008. The park is a stone's throw away from the family's Devon dairy farm. They have two children, Jake and Lily, and over 170 different species of birds and animals.

The Meerkats of Summer Farm

The True Story of Two Orphaned Meerkats
and the Family Who Saved Them

JAYNE COLLIER

sphere

SPHERE

First published in Great Britain in 2011 by Sphere
Reprinted 2011

A CIP catalogue record for this book
is available from the British Library.

ISBN 978-0-7515-4584-5

Typeset in Melior by M Rules
Printed and bound in Great Britain by
Clays Ltd, St Ives plc

Sphere
An imprint of
Little, Brown Book Group
100 Victoria Embankment
London EC4Y 0DY

An Hachette UK Company
www.hachette.co.uk

www.littlebrown.co.uk

To Andrew, who has the patience of a saint and is my best friend, and to Lily Mae and Jake Eli, who we are both immensely proud of. Love always.

Contents

Introduction

It was a grey and frosty February morning in Devon. As I walked towards Ringo's enclosure, gearing up for our daily battle, I looked up at the dark, foreboding skies and muttered a little prayer for good weather. It didn't look promising, but I always hope for a clear day that will bring visitors flocking through the gates of the park.

As usual, I could hear Ringo's indignant squawks before I saw him – he knew it was breakfast time and didn't appreciate being made to wait. And sure enough there he was, pressed up against the fence with his beady eyes glaring right at me. But however cross Ringo looks, it's hard to take him seriously: he's a grey-crowned crane, with goggly blue eyes and a black pom-pom on his head that wouldn't look out of place on a wedding guest. What he lacks in dignity, however, he more than makes up for in volume. Before I unlocked the gate to his enclosure, I picked up the dustbin lid that serves as a shield and then ventured in, his bowl of fruit in my hand. Ringo charged straight at me with his usual enthusiasm, desperate to get to his food and never mind my fingers. I fended him off as best I could with my anti-crane device, quickly picked up the scant remains of yesterday's dinner, dropped off his breakfast and hotfooted it out of there. I'm very fond of Ringo, but I avoid hanging around in his pen for any longer than absolutely necessary.

With Ringo temporarily pacified, I walked the familiar path to the next pen. I was on autopilot, carrying out the early-morning routine in a daze and dreaming, as I do every day, of the warm and cosy bed I'd left behind. Anyone in their right mind would still be tucked up on a morning like this, not fighting with bad-tempered birds! I stopped off at our little food shed, picked up another bowl of fruit and headed over to the meerkats' enclosure. At least this would be a more civilized experience. As I opened the door – no need for protection this time – I immediately noticed something odd. There were three small bundles scattered around the floor of the enclosure. What on earth? I put down the bowl and went to investigate the one nearest to me, a feeling of unease in the pit of my stomach. As I crouched down to look, my heart was in my mouth – I had this sense that something was terribly wrong, but what I saw still came as a complete shock: a tiny newborn meerkat, completely blind and without a speck of fur to keep it warm. What was it doing out here alone? And why wasn't it moving?

Would You Like a Pair of Wallabies?

It's two-and-a-half years since my husband Andrew and I officially opened the gates to Axe Valley Bird and Animal Park, which we built on the land next to our farmhouse in Kilmington, Devon. I can hardly believe it – the time really has flown by. Today we have twenty-seven species of animal, 150 species of bird and we have a regular stream of visitors through the gates. When I look back at where we started from ... well, it's hard to take it all in. It all began, as so many crazy plans do, with a 'What if ...' conversation, and if you'd told me then that all the schemes we plotted – late at night, after the children had gone to bed – would one day become a reality, never mind a success, I would have said you were mad.

The Meerkats of Summer Farm

Andrew and I are Devon born and bred, and both from a farming background. We grew up in close-knit families, surrounded by beautiful countryside and with animals – cats, dogs, chickens, sheep and cows – as a normal part of our daily lives. It's only as I've got older that I've come to realise how lucky we were as children, and how many people long for the life we took for granted. It seemed natural to both of us to recreate this sort of life for our own family, so the question of moving away and doing something else – working 9-to-5 in an office in town – never really came up. We're happy to continue the family tradition, and just hope that our children, Jake, who is twelve, and Lily, fourteen, enjoy the country life as much as we do.

My family's farm wasn't a large one – we had a small beef herd, about one hundred pigs and geese and chickens which we raised to sell. I have two younger brothers, Duncan and Nick, and we always helped around the farm – one of my most treasured family photos is of me and my dad when I was about six years old, walking up a country lane. I am carrying a huge bucket of horse feed, almost bigger than I am, and my dad, Alan, is on crutches after breaking his leg playing football. Like many girls I was really into horses when I was younger and I was lucky enough to have a beautiful pony named Silver who was my absolute pride and joy. I took such pleasure in grooming her and looking after all her tack and I have many lovely memories of riding her around the country lanes near my parents' farm. If Lily and Jake can carry memories like this with them into adulthood, then I'll be very happy.

Andrew's family have farmed in the area for years – his grandparents bought the farm that his parents went on to run and then they moved to Summer Farm, just one mile away from where Andrew was born, about twenty years ago. They have a small dairy herd which his dad, Mike, who is in his late sixties now, still looks after every day. His mum, Jill, used to do the local milk round when Andrew and his sisters Trudy and Emma were small, delivering to the village come rain or come shine.

Andrew's interest in birds can be traced right back to childhood – he'd always been keen on the ducks and chickens they had around the farm, but what really ignited his passion was when the family vet, Tim, gave him a duckling as a present. Andrew, aged only about eight or nine, loved that duckling and took real care of it, watching it grow ... and grow and grow and grow. He just couldn't understand why it was so much bigger than all the other ducks at the farm and kept asking Tim if he was absolutely *sure* it was a duck. Oh yes, said Tim with authority, definitely. Whether or not Andrew's mum and dad cottoned on to the fact that his duck was actually a goose before Andrew did, they'll never say. Needless to say, Tim had been pulling his leg all along. Olly the goose (named after Tim's son) went on to live happily with the family for years, eventually dying of old age. I'm sure he'd be very proud to know about the role he played in the origins of Axe Valley Bird and Animal Park!

Of course, I can't say that I never flirted with the idea of living somewhere a bit more cosmopolitan, or working in a job where I didn't have to wear wellies every day. After I left school, before I was married, I worked for a bank in our nearest town and for a few years I was quite content there. I made some good friends, had my own car and a weekly wage, and I enjoyed the feeling of being a real grown-up, with more freedom than I'd ever had before. But something about working indoors all day didn't agree with me, and I began to get ill. I was twenty-one when I decided I needed to leave for the sake of my health, and I went to work at a local garden centre, helping out in the shop and at the small café. I knew straight-away that I'd made the right choice – I loved talking to the customers and being out and about in the fresh air. Little did I know then that some of the skills I picked up there would prove to be extremely helpful later in life.

Andrew also had his own adventures before we were married. He trained as a gamekeeper at a local agricultural college and then worked at the Bindon estate in Axmouth for two years. He's the real nature enthusiast in our family, and loves nothing more than spending all day in the great outdoors – come rain or shine. I can only imagine how much he would have hated working in the bank! He learnt so much during that period, and to this day continues to amaze me with his knowledge of our local wildlife and his skill with all the weird and wonderful animals who now cross our paths. You know that scene in *Crocodile Dundee* where he calms down the angry dog just by staring at it and doing that thing with his hand? I'm not saying that Andrew could *definitely* do that … but I wouldn't be surprised!

We were married when we were twenty-four, in a marquee in one of our fields, having been together since I was eighteen years old. We met at our local branch of the Young Farmers' Club, and – corny as it might sound – we both knew from the beginning that one day we'd be married. We broke up briefly at one point, because Andrew was convinced we were too young to be as serious as we were, but soon got back together and have rarely spent a night apart since. When you work as hard as we do, it's so important to be a good team and to make each other laugh, which we do – every day.

You won't be surprised to hear that it was Andrew who first started the 'What if …' conversation. I can't remember exactly when or how it first came up, but I know we were living at Summer Farm in the house we've called home since we were married. After our wedding we moved into one half of Andrew's mum and dad's lovely farmhouse to help out with the herd. It's an arrangement that works really well – in spite of what you might think about living in such close proximity to your in-laws! The house is big enough to accommodate us all comfortably, and it's been properly divided into two so that we both have our own independent homes: me, Andrew, Jake and Lily on one side; Andrew's parents on the other. Jake and Lily love having their grandparents so close, and I must admit that having ready-made babysitters next door has proved very handy on more than one occasion. My mum and dad live just a few miles up the road, so there's never any shortage of family around.

So, as I said, I can't remember exactly when Andrew first floated the idea of us opening an animal park, but I imagine the scene went something like this . . .

Evening. A young couple sit down at the kitchen table with a pot of tea. The washing up's been done and the children are in bed. Everything is peaceful.

Husband: I saw a Water Rail down on the
River Yarty today.

Wife: [*Not really listening.*] Oh, really?

Husband: Yeah ... haven't seen one of those
beauties in a good few years. Not
many of them around anymore.

Wife: Mmm hmm.

Husband: Someone should start a breeding
programme, don't you think? Try to
get the levels back up again.

Wife: [*Silent. She's thinking about what to
put in the children's sandwiches for
school tomorrow.*]

Husband: I wish we could do something like
that. All this land we've got ... we
could definitely put up a few
aviaries, start off with a couple of
barn owls. Whaddya think?

Wife: [*Looks up quickly.*] Huh?!

I reckon that's pretty much how it went – just a little
nugget of an idea that Andrew brought up from time to

time, whenever we started talking about our future. Of course I thought he was mad to begin with, but the more he talked about it, and the more enthusiastic he became, the more the whole crazy notion started to make sense to me. We loved birds and animals, and we both felt like we wanted to create something of our own that we could be proud of. And in the back of both our minds there was also a niggling anxiety: these days farming can be a precarious way of making a living, and having some extra money coming in wouldn't hurt. Before long, the idea began to take on a life of its own; we'd design the layout of our dream park on little scraps of paper, and come up with elaborate plans which would have needed a lottery win to fund them. In the end though, it took one simple thing to transform our plans from fantasy to reality. And no, we didn't win the lottery! Andrew's dad casually offered us the use of a paddock behind the farmhouse and with that extra piece of land, which was ours to do with what we wished, we were suddenly able to take the first steps towards implementing our grand plan.

I remember so clearly walking out into that paddock with Andrew, one sun-dappled morning, and planning exactly where all of the enclosures would stand. We walked the perimeter, stopping every few hundred yards to say, 'This is where we'll have the kiosk for teas and coffees,' or 'How about putting the chicken coop here?' We were so excited to be finally able to turn our dreams into a real working bird and animal park. The possibilities seemed endless. But of course, first we needed a little start-up cash, and here we received help from an unlikely volunteer. Well, I say volunteer … it was actually our much-loved Labrador, Amber. We set her up on a date with a fine-looking fellow who lived nearby, and lo and behold, she went on to oblige us with six gorgeous puppies. We kept one for ourselves – named Willow – and sold the rest to loving homes to raise some money.

The first task was to erect the perimeter fences, and we used our Amber money to buy the supplies we needed. We did all the work ourselves; there were no leftover funds to employ anyone else to help, and so we'd go out to the paddock whenever we had a spare minute and bang in a few posts, using our tractor to cart the materials around. We had a tatty piece of graph paper with everything mapped out on it, and worked round the clock to get the basic structures in place. Soon we had homes for pheasants, ducks and bantam hens, and I can't tell you how exciting it was to see these birds – nothing exotic, but ours – happily pottering around their enclosures. Inevitably the money we'd raised from selling the puppies quickly ran out, and we used little bits of cash from selling some of the birds we were breeding to buy additional materials and stock as and when we could. It quickly became apparent, however, that if we wanted to do this properly, we needed some serious money. It was time to call in the professionals.

We made an appointment with a small-business advisor at the local Business Link, and he advised us to apply for a loan from the Prince's Trust because I was still under thirty and therefore young enough to be eligible for their help. He gave us pages and pages of forms to fill in, and we left feeling hopeful but slightly daunted by the bureaucratic hurdles we were going to have to jump over. We sat at our kitchen table every night for a week, carefully filling in the forms, trying to explain all our plans in a way that would be sure to win them over. They seemed like the most important pieces of paper in the world. A few days later, I drove down to Kilmington, pulled up by the post box and, somewhat cautiously, deposited the neatly addressed envelope which contained all our forms, not to mention all our hopes and dreams. Now there was nothing for us to do but wait ...

From that moment onwards, neither Andrew nor I could sit still, waiting to hear whether our application had been successful. Every time the phone rang, we both jumped six feet in the air and scrambled to answer it as quickly as possible. Our friends and family must have been a little annoyed by the disappointed response they got whenever they called over those anxious few weeks. Then one day, finally, the call came. They wanted me to appear before a committee in Plymouth to explain our plans in person. Well! I didn't know whether to be excited or scared; happy or disappointed. I was so relieved they hadn't said no straight away, but the thought of having to wait even longer for an answer was almost unbearable. When the day of the interview finally came around, I stood in front of a panel of three serious-looking people – just like on *Dragons' Den* – dressed in my finest. They seemed completely terrifying, although I'm sure they were actually very kind to me. I had to explain how we saw the business developing, our plans for the future and how we planned to invest the money they – might – give us. I can't remember a word of what I said; I was mostly concentrating on not fainting and I was convinced they could hear my heart pounding.

It seemed like I was in there for hours, although in reality the interview only took about thirty minutes. I remember walking out of the building to meet Andrew and Mum in a complete daze, unable to answer any of their questions about what had happened inside. They'd been to visit the aquarium while I'd been going through the Spanish Inquisition, and had had a lovely old time of it, lucky things. Andrew turned to me as we walked away from the building and said, philosophically, that we'd done all we could and it was in their hands now. And no matter what their answer, we wouldn't give up on our plans. I knew he was right, but I couldn't quell my anxiety.

So much seemed to hang on their response. How on earth would we raise the money we needed if they said no?

Another period of anxious waiting followed. Poor Lily and Jake, who were only little at the time, must have wondered what on earth was going on! The wait seemed endless, and after a while I began to give up hope. I stopped jumping for the phone, or running to pick up the post every morning. I convinced myself that they weren't going to give us the money. Then, one day, a single white envelope landed on the mat. I eyed it suspiciously from a distance, as if it was a dangerous animal I needed to be wary of. It didn't look like a bill, and there were no birthdays approaching, so I realised that it must be from the Prince's Trust. It would be their standard rejection letter, surely. I picked it up with resignation, wondering whether I should go and fetch Andrew from the barn where he was working with his dad. No point, I thought, I can tell him the bad news at lunchtime. I leaned against the counter, opened the letter and scanned it quickly, looking for the words I knew in my heart of hearts would be there: 'I regret to inform you ... unsuccessful on this occasion ... blah blah blah'. But instead of the cursory couple of paragraphs I was expecting, there seemed to be several sheets, with a lengthy letter stapled to the front. I quickly read the opening few lines: 'Dear Mr and Mrs Collier, Thank you ... delighted to inform you ... successful ... £1000'.

'ANDREW!' I screamed, running out into the yard, waving the letter above my head like a madwoman. He came dashing out of the barn, looking worried.

'Jayne? What's wrong? Is something the matter?' he asked, obviously alarmed by my shrieks.

'No,' I gasped, out of breath with excitement. 'The letter ... it's here! See? £1000! They're giving us ONE THOUSAND POUNDS!' I pushed the letter in his face, gulping in great breaths of air and trying to calm down. He seized it from me, read the same few life-changing lines and then whooped out loud, grabbing me in a big bear hug and spinning me round.

'This is it, Jayne! What did I tell you? I never doubted we'd get the money for an instant!'

And that, indeed, was it. That £1000, and the help that the Prince's Trust gave us in planning for the future, really was the beginning of the Axe Valley Bird and Animal Park we know today.

Over the next few years, we added slowly but surely to the park. We mainly had birds to begin with, then a few rabbits, guinea pigs and other small animals. We made good use of two local vets, our old friend Tim and his colleague JJ, who kept our growing flock in good health, and we sold eggs, chickens and other birds to keep a small but steady trickle of cash coming in. We didn't open to the public immediately – for a long while, there wasn't all that much to see – but we'd show friends and family round the park and take pride in their compliments and enthusiastic responses to everything we'd built.

My greatest wish for the park, from the beginning, was to introduce a variety of animals to sit alongside the birds that Andrew loves so much. I just knew that if we wanted the visitors to come flooding in, we needed to provide plenty of cute and cuddly creatures for them to look at. I've always loved animals and walking out of my house every morning and being surrounded by a wild and wonderful menagerie was something I could only have dreamt about as a child. Of course, neither Andrew nor I were experts when it came to exotic animals, and I knew we'd have to do plenty of research before we even thought about bringing one into our lives. And how did you even go about getting your hands on a lemur, a meerkat or a raccoon? It's not as if we could just go down to the pet shop and buy one.

Luckily, Andrew was able to pick up some tips while working a few shifts at the local zoo. He is incredibly knowledgeable about British nature and wildlife, but had less experience with anything more unusual, so it was great for him to have the opportunity to work alongside the zookeepers and see the animals up close and personal. And the money he earned helped keep us going at the park. One day, one of the keepers, who must have heard about what we were up to at Axe Valley, sidled up to Andrew and asked him a question that would change our lives.

'Would you like a pair of wallabies?'

It turned out they had a pair at the zoo that they needed to move on, and what could be better than relocating them just a few miles down the road? Andrew called me straight away and asked what I thought. I didn't need to think about it at all. Without a thought of enclosures, food, or any other practical matters, I said yes. This snap decision would be repeated over the next few years, as more and more unusual animals came our way. We always seem to say 'yes' before we've even thought about where we're going to put the newcomers, or how we're going to feed them, and then we have to rush about like fools, building enclosures and researching their feeding and breeding habits. And that's just how it was that night, after Andrew came home: we pulled down the big encyclopaedia and looked up wallabies. Once we'd got the hang of the basics (Australian, smaller than a kangaroo) we called up Tim the vet and warned him about our new arrivals. He was shocked, but excited to have something other than a cow to look at for once. He promised he'd do some research and come by to visit once our new friends had arrived. Next, they needed a home. We walked up to the park and identified a spot where we thought they'd be happy. We spent the next few evenings sawing and hammering, making sure the fences were tall enough to keep them contained and that they'd have enough room to hop about freely. Finally, we were ready.

The wallabies arrived one Wednesday afternoon, and I remember standing in the drive with Lily and Jake, holding their hands as we waited for the truck from the zoo to arrive. Although the children were only eight and six years old, they were quite used to the regular influx of new birds at the park. They didn't think there was anything particularly exciting about the arrival of a new owl or a kestrel. But I'd explained to them that today we'd be getting something a bit different – two new animals, and not a boring old cat or dog. I'd shown them the pictures in the encyclopaedia, and they were *so* excited, hopping around like little wallabies themselves as we waited for the men from the zoo to arrive. Eventually the truck appeared, and I waved it in the direction of the park, where Andrew was waiting. Two men from the zoo got out, said a quick hello and then unloaded a cage from the back. Much to Lily and Jake's disappointment, it was covered by a cloth, and I could tell they were on the verge of reaching out their little fingers and whipping it away so that they could see the wallabies straight away. I sensed that wouldn't go down well with the zookeepers, so I held on to their hands tightly, and we all watched in eager anticipation as the cage was manoeuvred into the new enclosure and, finally, the cloth was removed. There, looking slightly bewildered, were two absolutely gorgeous creatures – much smaller than I'd imagined, and both covered in a shaggy coat that was quite different from that of the kangaroos I'd seen in zoos and on television. The keeper opened the door to the cage, and after a few minutes of anxious air-sniffing, the two wallabies hopped out cautiously, one after the other. We'd left a bowl of greens and fruit near to the cage and they quickly spotted it and started to nibble on the pieces of lettuce. We were all enthralled – even Jake and Lily, who'd been so full of noisy enthusiasm only minutes before, just stood and watched in rapt silence. I don't think any of us could believe that these wonderful animals would be living with us from now on. After a while, we tore ourselves away and left them alone to settle in. The zookeepers passed on a few final words of advice, climbed into their van and left. And then we were alone with a pair of wallabies ...

Of course, the wallabies – named Ruby and Clancy by Jake and Lily – were only the beginning. RJ, a hand-reared baby raccoon, followed soon after, then dastardly Ringo, and then our first meerkats, Mango and Tango. I've always had a soft spot for meerkats, and hoped that one day we'd be able to have a colony in the park. They're such funny creatures, almost like little people with their upright bodies and expressive faces. Anytime I've been to a zoo, the meerkats have always been one of the star attractions, and children in particular seem to be real fans of their comical antics.

Mango came to us through a piece of pure luck. I was reading the paper one day, checking out the classified ads like I always do, and my eyes immediately jumped past all the ads for puppies and kittens to the phrase MEERKAT FOR SALE. I reached for the phone straight away and called the number, worried that it might already have been sold. Luckily, the young female was still available, and I soon had my heart set on buying her. She was affordable, and even though we'd have to drive to Swindon to collect her it was such a rare opportunity that I didn't think we should pass it up. Thankfully Andrew agreed, and a few weekends later – having rapidly constructed a suitable meerkat enclosure – we set off to collect her. By this point I was getting used to that feeling of excitement mixed with nervousness that came every time we met a new animal, but this time it seemed even stronger. I think because meerkats have always been a particular favourite of mine, I was nervous about being disappointed. Thankfully, I needn't have worried. Mango, as the children had already decided to call her, was just beautiful. She had a lithe, sandy-coloured body with darker patterns along her back and around her eyes. She was wary of us, and didn't like to be handled, but was clearly a lively and happy young thing. I couldn't wait to get her home.

Meerkats are sociable creatures by nature, usually living in 'gangs' or 'mobs' of around twenty, all of whom have their assigned roles within the group. I knew we'd have to find Mango a mate as soon as possible so that we could begin to create our own little meerkat society. Thankfully, it wasn't too long before we were able to find her a boyfriend – Tango, of course – who came from a park in Cornwall. They got on like a house on fire from the moment we introduced them, and it wasn't long before we had a crowd of baby meerkats to contend with. They had a magnificent enclosure, filled with sand for burrowing in, pipes to mimic the underground tunnels they live in in the wild, and a huge, gnarly tree trunk which Andrew found one day after a particularly violent storm. They love to clamber all over this, and use it as their favourite lookout spot. Mango was a wonderful mother to her first litter – always playing with them and patiently letting them climb on her. It was such a joy to sit and watch them all together – once we had a reasonable-sized gang, you could see the meerkats beginning to carry out their designated roles, just as they would in the wild. They'd take it in turns to act as sentry – usually for about an hour each – standing alert at all times on the highest point in the enclosure and letting all the others know when we were approaching.

The Meerkats of Summer Farm

Meerkats can carry up to four litters in one year, but I had no idea that Mango was pregnant again. And she'd been so wonderful with her first litter that I assumed that when the next one arrived, she'd be just as dedicated. So when that cold February morning came around, and I discovered the abandoned litter in her pen, I was completely taken aback. What on earth could have happened? Why would she reject these babies? But I didn't have time to dwell on these questions; there would be time for that later. It was so bitterly cold outside, and I knew the pups were in real danger of freezing. Without stopping to wonder if it was the right thing to do, I let my instinct take over and picked up the three tiny babies, placing them gently in the pocket of my coat. I rushed back to the house as quickly as I could, eager to get them inside, into the warmth, and see what I could do to save them.

Meerkats on the Aga

I ran into the kitchen, almost tripping over Amber in my haste. What could I use to warm the babies? Ideally they should be placed in a specialist incubator to raise their temperature, but I needed something I could put to use straight away. I thought of calling Tim for advice, but I didn't want to waste any more time. Who knew how long they'd already been out there in the cold? Suddenly, I had a flash of inspiration and knew just what to do. The Aga! Like many traditional farmhouses, our kitchen is heated by an old range, and we do all of our cooking on there. Throughout winter it emits a gentle, comforting heat and it is a favourite spot for Amber and Willow's regular naps. I carefully wrapped the three babies in a tea towel for protection, checked the stove wasn't too hot and laid them gently on the top. I only hoped it would be enough to save them. I could just see their tiny, pink chests quivering, proving to me that they were still alive, but their skin was icy to the touch and I feared I was too late.

Whenever I tell this story – and over the last year I've told it a lot – someone always asks if I was worried about the meerkats cooking on top of the Aga. Honestly? No, I wasn't. I suppose it might have been a risk if the stove had been hotter, but I knew from experience that it was cool enough to touch and that with some protection from the towel I'd wrapped them in, the heat it gave off was the best chance of saving them. For added safety I dug out an old fingerless glove and gently placed each baby inside, hoping that the extra layer would help stave off the cold. They were so small that they each fitted inside one of the glove's fingers.

Having done all I could to protect the babies from the most immediate danger – the cold – I sat down in the chair to think what I needed to do next. My heart was still racing with adrenalin and I wasn't at all sure I'd done the right thing. What if Mango's 'abandonment' of her babies was only temporary, and she came back later to find them gone? I knew enough about animals to know that with my scent on them, the babies could never be returned to their mother. I couldn't help worrying I'd made a terrible mistake. Andrew was due back from taking the kids to school any moment, and I knew he'd have some good advice, and in the meantime I could make that call to the vet. Tim, used by now to getting unusual calls from Axe Valley, took my news in his stride and reassured me that the babies would undoubtedly have died if I'd left them out there any longer, whether or not Mango intended to return to them. Getting them into the warmth was the best way to save them. As we spoke, I walked over to the Aga and took another look at my new charges. Was it just me or were they starting to look a bit healthier? Was that one even wriggling a bit? Tim suggested I try feeding them with some kitten milk from a syringe. Andrew and I have both done our fair share of hand-rearing animals over the years, so I was familiar with the routine, but I wasn't sure that we'd have a syringe small enough to feed the meerkats. Tim said he'd bring one round later, and in the meantime I found some kitten milk – thankfully we had some left over from our most recent litter – and tried to get the babies to take some off my finger. My feelings of anxiety were slowly beginning to melt away, replaced by butterflies of excitement – I couldn't wait for Andrew to get home. Happily, two of the babies were definitely perking up and seemed to manage a little of the milk from my finger. But no matter what I did, one of them still seemed to be struggling and didn't seem interested in the milk at all. I covered her with an extra layer of towel, in case she was still cold, and held my milky finger right up to her minuscule mouth. Nothing. I pulled a stool up to the Aga and watched over them all, carefully. The other two were really wriggly, pushing each other out of the way in an attempt to get closer to the milk, but this little one continued to lie there, showing no signs of improvement. I watched her closely, willing her to survive, but even as I sat and stared, I could see the tremulous movement in her chest begin to slow. The next minute, she was gone. I sighed; you don't grow up on a farm without becoming used to animals dying, but I was sorry that I hadn't been able to do anything to help this little baby, who'd had such a rotten start in life. I lifted her off the Aga and put her to one side – she would have a proper burial later. It was time to turn my attention to the two healthy ones and make absolutely sure that they survived.

I heard the rumble of Andrew's Land Rover outside, and hurried to the back door. As soon as he got out of the car, I started calling him inside – sometimes he heads straight over to the park, and I didn't want to miss him.

'Andrew, come into the kitchen ... quickly! I've got something to show you.' I was practically bouncing up and down with excitement. He looked puzzled, but headed straight in, Willow hot on his heels. Once in the kitchen, he stood there expectantly, waiting for me to tell him what was going on.

'Over there. Look! On the Aga.'

Shooting me a confused look, he walked over to the stove and peered into the tea-towel. He leant forward to get a better look, then shot straight up again in surprise.

'Jayne! What on earth *are* they?'

He was right to be confused. The baby meerkats, to be fair, did look like pretty much every other baby animal I've ever seen: pink, blind and wriggly. I quickly filled him in on the morning's drama and he shook his head, bewildered. 'I wonder what made Mango reject these babies? I suppose we'll never know.' He pulled back the towel covering the babies to get a closer look. Andrew might have been a touch bemused to find baby meerkats asleep on our stove, but I knew he was too much of an animal lover not to be immediately fascinated by them. We discussed the best way to keep the babies alive over these next few critical hours, agreeing that one of us should stay with them for the rest of the day and we should try to get them to eat as much as possible.

Just as Andrew was getting over the shock, Tim arrived with some extra supplies of kitten milk and a tiny syringe for feeding the babies. He checked them over and told us they seemed to be in reasonably good health. He left us with a warning that if we intended to hand-rear these meerkats ourselves, we'd better be prepared for a few sleepless nights: they needed feeding *every two hours*. It was a daunting thought, being responsible for these defenceless little creatures. We knew they would rely on us for everything, in a way that the other animals in the park never had. One of us would always have to be watching them – at least for the first few weeks – and with the park and Jake and Lily to look after, would we have the time and the energy? I gazed down at the pathetic little things and felt my heart swell. Having brought them this far, there's no way I could give them to someone else to look after. They were mine. I looked at Andrew, and I knew he was having the same debate in his head. Suddenly, he looked at me and said, 'You know what? Maybe it's madness to try and hand-rear these babies ourselves ... but wasn't it madness to buy a wallaby when we'd only ever had cows and chickens before? We'll figure it out, just like we always do. And the kids will help.'

I smiled. It was true, Jake and Lily would be so excited to meet the babies. They were good, responsible children and they were old enough to pitch in and help. 'OK, let's do it!' I said, already getting up to prepare another feed. Together we figured out how to use the little syringe, filled it with milk and used it to squirt teeny droplets into the babies' gaping mouths. Although a fair amount seemed to end up on their faces, I could already tell they had healthy appetites and I was delighted to see them squirming around and squeaking with glee as they gulped down their milk.

A few hours – and several feeds – later, Lily and Jake came charging in through the door, with Andrew bringing up the rear. Clearly he'd already broken the exciting news on the ride back from school. 'Mum! Where are they?' Lily squealed in excitement, throwing her schoolbag down on the floor. Her brother was only marginally less giddy, hopping from one foot to the other.

'Where's who?' I asked, innocently.

'Mu-um!' wailed Jake. 'The meerkats! Dad told us. Where are they?'

I laughed – their enthusiasm was infectious – and pointed in the direction of the Aga. 'But be careful,' I warned. 'They're very fragile.' Skidding to a rapid halt in front of the stove, Lily peeled back the towel, almost reverentially, and peeped inside. Jake was right by her side.

'Wow ... Mum, they're so tiny!' he whispered. 'How old do you think they are?'

'They can only have been a few hours old when I found them,' I said. 'They weren't in the enclosure last night.'

'Can I touch one?' Lily asked, nervously.

'You can feed them if you like, as long as you're very gentle.'

Their eyes lit up, and I showed them how to fill the syringe with milk and carefully squeeze the droplets into the hungry meerkats' open mouths. I've rarely seen my children so quiet as they watched the babies – their appetites temporarily sated – settle down for a nap. They were entranced, and for the rest of the evening they hung over the box where we'd now placed the babies, watching them intently. They were even more reluctant than usual to go upstairs and do their homework. I let them do one more feed before bed, and we all stood around the box and watched with delight as the meerkats squirmed and squeaked. They were so lively now, and looked like normal, healthy babies. I could hardly believe that only a few hours earlier they'd been so close to death.

As I sent Jake and Lily up to bed, I said to them, 'You two can have the honour of naming the babies. I want you both to have a good think about it and let me know tomorrow what you've agreed.' And with that important task to occupy them, they both dashed upstairs as if it was Christmas Eve – they'd already figured out that the sooner they went to sleep, the sooner it would be morning and time for them to feed the meerkats again.

As Andrew has to get up very early to help his father with the milking, I volunteered to feed the babies during the night. To be honest, I was actually looking forward to it. I already felt a strong attachment to my tiny charges, and I was determined that they should have plenty of love and attention to make up for their rocky start in life. I went to bed at eleven, and set my alarm clock to 1 a.m. for the first feed.

BEEP! BEEP! BEEP!

The alarm screeched, insistently. I sat bolt upright in bed, shocked by the loud and unexpected intrusion into my deep and dreamless sleep. Then I remembered: the meerkats. OK, so now I wasn't quite so excited about the late-night feeds. But, with a resentful glance at Andrew's slumbering back – he'll sleep through anything – I pulled on my dressing gown, shoved my feet into my slippers and headed downstairs.

The kitchen was pitch black, and as I fumbled for the light switch I felt something furry brush past my legs. I jumped and hit the switch, only to see Amber staring up at me, her big brown eyes confused, as if to say, 'What are you doing here at this ungodly hour? Is it time for my breakfast?' I gave her a pat on the head, mumbling 'Good girl', and blinking in the bright lights. I suddenly remembered nighttime feeds with Jake and Lily, and that same sense of bleary disorientation. Nevertheless, I had cherished that time with them, and the feeling that we were the only people in the world as I rocked them back and forth in the early hours of the morning. They were both such good babies, and even though I went through all the usual first-time mum worries with Lily, I had my own mum on-hand to help me, and Andrew was very involved, so I really enjoyed those early months with both children.

The meerkats were now in a covered box on the counter, still close to the Aga for warmth, but safe from the prying noses of Amber and Willow, or worse, our cats Tarka and Blue. As I went over to check on them, I felt a sudden sense of unease. What if something had happened to them while we'd been asleep? What if they'd taken a turn for the worse? Gingerly, I pulled back the towel which covered them and breathed a sigh of relief when I saw them cuddled up together, sleeping peacefully. Sleeping peacefully until I disturbed them, that is. They were soon squeaking away, eager for the milk they'd already figured out was coming their way. I sat at the kitchen table with their box on my knee and squeezed the milk into their yawning mouths. Or maybe it was me who was yawning. One seemed to be more confident than the other, and nudged his brother out of the way to get to the milk first. I could see I'd have to keep an eye on that one! It didn't take much to fill their little tummies, and they were soon settling down for another snooze, curling up together in a ball. I tucked them back in, stopped by Willow and Amber's basket to give them both a proper stroke, and then turned out the light. 'See you in two hours, guys.'

One night feed down; only two more to go before morning.

Wren and Rascal

'Come up with any good names yet, kids?' I asked the next morning, as everyone rushed around getting ready for school and the day ahead.

'Not yet,' sighed Jake. 'I think maybe we need to get to know them a bit more first.'

Lily was spooning cereal into her mouth, standing over the meerkats' box and watching them closely. 'That one's definitely the boss,' she said, pointing to the fellow I'd noticed elbowing his brother out of the way last night. (If meerkats have elbows, that is.) I went over to look, and saw the 'boss' had taken the prime spot in the box, nearest to the old cuddly-toy penguin we'd given them to snuggle up to. 'He's a bit of a rascal, that's for sure,' I agreed. Lily's eyes instantly lit up.

'Rascal! That's what we should call him. It's the perfect name. Well done, Mum!'

I thought about it for a moment. 'Rascal ... it does have a nice ring to it. And it definitely suits him. Jake, what do you think?'

'I think it's cool. But what about the other one? He needs a name, too. Maybe it should be something else beginning with "R"?'

We all sat and thought for a moment, and then I had a sudden moment of inspiration. My brother Duncan's spaniel had recently had a litter of puppies, and they had decided to keep one for themselves. They'd really struggled to decide on a suitable name though, and being used to coming up with inventive animal names at short notice, they asked for our help. I suggested 'Wren' and they all loved it – the little puppy had his new name. I was so pleased with my idea that I was secretly a bit sad that I hadn't saved it for one of our animals! Maybe we could recycle it for Rascal's little brother?

'What about Wren?' I asked the children, as they shrugged on their coats and headed towards the door. 'It doesn't exactly begin with an "R", but it does go well with Rascal, and I think it suits the little chap.'

'Wren and Rascal.' Jake tried it out for size as we all headed to the car. 'I like it!'

After I'd dropped the children off at the station in Axminster, where the bus picks them up for school, I drove the six miles to Lyme Regis to visit our friend Richard. He runs a fruit and veg shop and really helps us out by putting aside all the fruit that's past its sell-by date and that he can no longer display. I pick up a huge plastic bin of fruit every couple of days and it goes a long way towards feeding our hungry menagerie. I can't begin to imagine how much money we'd have to spend on fresh produce if he wasn't so generous. Today was a particularly good day, and there were tons of bananas – only slightly brown – and a great pile of kiwis and grapes. Thanks to Richard, the animals would be well fed today.

Back at the house, I checked in on Wren and Rascal, who were already squeaking and ready for their next feed. I realised that until we got into the swing of these regular feeds, I was going to need some help. And I knew just who to ask. Picking up the phone, I dialled a familiar number.

'Mum? It's me. I was wondering if you could do me a favour ...?'

My lovely mum, Val, learnt a long time ago to expect unusual animal-related calls from me, and took the news about the meerkats in her stride. She's pretty unflappable. She agreed to come down to the park and help out with the feeding so that I'd be able to nip back to the house at regular intervals to check on the babies and do their feeds. Mum is such a great help: she knows the whole routine at the park and we can always rely on her to lend a hand whenever we're stretched. We usually manage to get away for a week's break when the park is quiet – which tends to be in November – and Mum always steps in to look after the animals for us. Of course it's wonderful to get away as a family, but we can't help but worry that something will happen while we're not there and so we never go anywhere that we can't drive back from quickly – our current favourite is the Center Parcs resort at Longleat Forest in Wiltshire.

Feeling relieved that help was en route, I fed the

babies and then headed out for the park. Ever since we opened to the public, the daily routine has been pretty similar. The gates open at 10 a.m. and I try to make sure all of the animals are fed and watered before then. Andrew takes care of all the daily maintenance – there's always something which needs hammering back into place, or an enclosure which needs expanding – and I do all the feeding. The two of us keep an eye on the entrance gate, and are usually both on-hand to answer any questions that visitors might have. We never know how many people will visit the park on any given day – we had about fifty people through the gates on that first day two-and-a-half years ago (boosted by plenty of friends and family) and now we average around twenty-five most days. On one memorable day we had forty-five people through the gates – a record for us – which was really exciting. Luckily we can see the little car park and entrance gate from the house, so sometimes – on a quiet day – we can both escape to the house for lunch or a cuppa, and still sprint over to the park when we see a car approaching.

I hauled the bin of fruit into the little shed where I

do all of the food prep and set about getting the first few meals prepared before Mum came. Our animals all have different dietary requirements, so I prepare each meal individually. There's lots of chopping involved, and I'm quite the whizz with a knife these days. We buy frozen chicks and sprats in bulk, and keep a freezer stocked with these for our carnivorous inhabitants. First on my agenda today were Mango and Tango and the rest of their brood; I wanted to check how they were and whether there were any signs of distress after yesterday's drama. I prepared a lovely bowl of fruit and dried dog biscuits, making sure there were lots of grapes in there — their favourite.

The usual cacophony assailed me as I walked towards their enclosure. I could hear Ringo, of course, but the otters, Max and Millie, were also chiming in with their own relentlessly ear-splitting squeaks. There really is no other noise like it in the world, and I've often had concerned visitors rushing up to me, telling me that they think our otters are hurt or in distress. No, they're just hungry, I tell them. And loud! I've got used to the medley of different squawks,

squeals, grunts and growls now. I think I'd be worried
if I walked into the park to complete silence. Then I'd
know something was really wrong.

Mango and Tango's pen was a hive of activity.
Thanks to Wren and Rascal I was a bit later on my
rounds today, and they'd already emerged from their
burrows and were scampering all over the big tree
trunk which dominates their home. When the sentry
on lookout duty, standing erect and proud on the
trunk's highest branch, heard me coming, he barked
out a warning and the whole gang scarpered into the
tunnels. I opened the gate as quietly as I could and
stepped inside, scanning the ground for any more
unusual surprises. Nothing, thankfully. I put the bowl
of fruit down, moved a few feet away and crouched
down to wait for them to re-emerge. They're not tame,
and won't be handled, but if I'm quiet and still
enough they will go about their business with me in
the pen – particularly at feeding time. After a few
minutes, Tango poked his head cautiously out of one
of the tunnels – he must have been the sentry; they're
always the first to reappear. He slowly emerged, and
having passed the message back to the rest of the

family that there was no danger, they all followed him out. I sat and watched for a while as they gathered round the food bowl and tucked into the fruit. Everyone seemed OK and their behaviour was completely normal. I watched Mango particularly closely, but couldn't see any signs that she was missing her babies. I stayed for a few moments longer, then headed out. I'd never know exactly what happened to Wren and Rascal, but at least everyone seemed to be healthy and happy.

By the time I headed back to get the next meal ready – it had better be the otters', or they'd raise the whole neighbourhood – I saw Mum at the tea and coffee kiosk, fixing herself a cuppa. When she saw me, she raised her hand in greeting and gestured to the kettle. Did I want one? I nodded, and went to wash my hands before going to join her. I took a seat on one of the picnic benches, noticing that Mum had already put some fresh wildflowers in the vase on each table. She brought the cups over, and set them down on the table along with a Tupperware box. I knew there was bound to be some sort of tasty treat inside – Mum used to be a cook in a local restaurant, and often bakes traditional Devonshire scones or other cakes and biscuits which we sell in the kiosk.

'So,' she said, opening the box and revealing a pile of freshly baked brownies, 'meerkat babies. Whatever next?'

I smiled, taking a cake. 'I know. It's mad. But Mum, you should have seen them. I couldn't just leave them out there. They would have died.'

'You always were a soft-hearted thing,' Mum said, fondly. 'But you said from the beginning that you wanted to breed your meerkats, so what else could you have done?'

I nodded in agreement, and told her all about the previous day's crazy events. She shook her head in amazement when I told her about their feeding sched-ule. 'So it's going to be all hands on deck around here for a while then?'

'Looks like it. You don't mind doing some of the feeds in the park, do you?' I knew she'd be only too happy to help, but she brought me up well and I know it's only polite to ask! She assured me that she'd be delighted to step in whenever she could, and with that went off to pacify the otters. I stayed to finish my tea, but then heard the rumble of an engine and turned to see a car pull up – the first visitors of the day. I cleared up our tea things and went to greet them. We charge a deliberately low fee for entrance because we want people to feel like they're getting good value for money and to come back again – and to recommend us to their friends. It seems to be working, and our numbers are definitely going up, slowly but surely. In the very early days, before we were fully opened, we had an honesty box, but I'm afraid to say that it didn't work out too well! Once we'd sifted out all the euros, buttons and other random paraphernalia, we weren't exactly making much of a profit, so we decided we'd better make things a bit more formal. Once I'd let the visitors in, I wandered back to the house, confident that Mum would handle whatever came up at the park.

In contrast to the previous day, it was lovely outside. Bright and crisp, and the view from the garden across the valley was beautiful. I paused for a moment to take it all in. The gentle rumble of machinery from the farm, where Andrew was working with his dad. The distant sound of Mum chatting to the visitors, probably offering them one of her brownies. I leant on the fence, grateful for this brief moment of peace and solitude. I have chosen a life that is full, from the moment I get out of bed in the morning, until I fall into it again at night, exhausted. There is always something to do; someone or something to feed. I wouldn't have it any other way, and I know how lucky I am to live a life I enjoy so very much. Moments for reflection are rare, and I think that means I value them even more. The events of the past twenty-four hours flashed through my mind. I was so proud of the way everyone in the family had risen to the challenge, accepting these vulnerable creatures into our lives – and all the disruption that came with them – without question. That we were able to take care of these little babies made me really happy, and proved that what we were doing at the park was worthwhile.

'Jayne!' A shout interrupted my reverie. It was Andrew, standing outside the house. I saw that Tim's car was pulling up and remembered that he'd offered to come back today, having spent the previous night consulting his veterinary books. I set off for the house, eager to hear what he'd learnt about meerkat babies.

A few hours later I felt like a bona fide meerkat expert – Tim had really come through for us. He'd managed to get hold of a proper 'zoo-zone box', and Wren and Rascal were now safely housed in a sturdy new home with a secure mesh lid that we could watch them through. He told us to keep up the kitten-milk feeds every two hours for about six weeks until they were ready to move onto solids. Apparently meerkat young learn how to forage for food by mimicking the adults in their gang, so we'd have to find a way to teach Wren and Rascal ourselves. Although we'd be providing their food, we wanted them to behave as naturally as possible.

The more Tim told us, the more I was reminded what remarkable creatures meerkats are. In the wild, an adult meerkat will teach a baby how to hunt and kill a venomous scorpion by catching one itself and then removing the sting, so the young meerkat can practise hunting safely. Isn't that amazing? They're the only species to have been observed doing this.

There's one thing Tim told us which wasn't quite so appealing. Apparently it takes baby meerkats a while to learn how to wee and poo on their own, and their mothers have to stimulate these functions by licking them in the necessary areas. Well, fond as I already was of little Wren and Rascal, there was no way I was going to be licking their nether regions! We decided to see if using a cloth would work as well, and I tentatively dabbed at their bottoms. They were still so small that I was frightened of hurting them, and my ineffectual dabbing didn't seem to be doing anything. In the end I had to be a bit more forceful, which luckily had the desired effect.

'No greater love, Wren,' I whispered to the tiny creature as he pooed in my hand. 'No greater love!'

Thinking Outside the Box

Over the next few weeks we settled into a routine with Wren and Rascal. I was still their main care-taker – their surrogate mum, I suppose – but everyone pitched in to lend a hand, and there was no shortage of visitors to the house, eager to meet our new arrivals.

Jake and Lily would take it in turns to do the first feed of the day before they went to school. I was really impressed with how seriously they were taking their responsibilities, and touched to see how ten-derly they looked after Wren and Rascal. Mum came over most days to help open up the park and do some of the feeding, which left me free to do the meerkats' feeds during the day and to play with Wren and

Rascal, who were becoming increasingly lively. They liked to be tickled and were soon standing up – in that famous meerkat pose – to have their tummies stroked. By now they both had a light covering of hair, and their eyes had opened, but they were still pretty tiny, only a few inches long. Andrew was out and about in the park or on the farm most of the time, but he'd stop by the house a few times a day to play with the babies or give them a feed, and when Jake and Lily came home from school, they were back in charge. That was when I usually managed to find a few minutes to sit down and put my feet up. I was pretty exhausted after two weeks of regular night feeds, I can tell you.

When Wren and Rascal were about a month old, we decided it was time to let them out of the box to get some exercise on the kitchen floor. And that's when the real fun began. I'd always been nervous about the dogs' and cats' reactions to these furry interlopers, and had watched their behaviour around Wren and Rascal very carefully. I knew the babies were safe when the lid was on their box, but as long as I was in the kitchen, I liked to leave the lid off so that they weren't shut up all the time. That was when I kept a very close eye on Willow, Amber, Blue and Tarka. From day one, they were extremely intrigued by this strange box that had appeared in the kitchen: their territory. They would sniff around it suspiciously, and once or twice I caught Blue swatting gently at the lid with his claw. They soon lost interest though, and seemed happy to leave the box alone – as long as they were still being fed and petted regularly, which they certainly were, then they were content. But I was sure it would be an entirely different matter when I started letting Wren and Rascal out to run around; I could just imagine Blue or Tarka mistaking one of the babies for a mouse, and then having to stand by helplessly as they were pursued around the kitchen. I decided that, at least to begin with, it would be safest to shut the cats and dogs out of the kitchen before letting the babies out.

I thought it would be best to attempt Wren and Rascal's first 'outside' adventure when there was no one else around. I didn't know how they'd react, and I didn't want anything to alarm them. I carefully lifted their box down onto the floor, took off the lid and gently lifted them out. I placed them on the flag-stones, next to their box, and then sat on the floor, cross-legged, to watch. To begin with, they seemed nervous of the vast expanse of kitchen floor, and the unexplored terrain of the cold flagstones. They stayed close to the safety of the box, and each other. Then Rascal, ever the boss, started to venture slightly fur-ther afield, with Wren sticking close to his heels. They both scampered towards me, and sniffed around my shoes; I imagine they were comforted by my familiar smell. It was amazing to watch them taking their first real steps into the big wide world. I wonder what was going through their minds? A traditional Devonshire farmhouse kitchen was certainly a very different terrain to the Kalahari Desert – where meerkats live in the wild – or even to the slightly-less-wild meerkat habitat at Axe Valley Bird and Animal Park. Their little claws scrabbled around on the smooth floor, looking for purchase ... something to dig into, as is their natural instinct.

I gave Wren a little stroke on his head and he turned to me, his intelligent eyes staring straight into mine, as if to say, 'I'm not sure about this, Jayne. I think I'd like to go back in the box now.' Rascal had discovered he could dig at the grouting in between the flagstones, and before he could do too much damage, I picked them both up, gave them a quick cuddle, and then put them back into the safety of their box, where they immediately snuggled up to their penguin and fell asleep, worn out by their big adventure.

With that first expedition under their belts, Wren and Rascal seemed to grow in confidence, exploring the deepest, darkest corners of the kitchen every time I let them out of the box. When they were six weeks old, I started putting small pieces of fruit, mealworms and bits of dog biscuit on the floor, and encouraged the babies to eat them. The sooner they were on solids, the sooner I'd be able to get back to something approaching a normal routine! It reminded me of trying to wean Jake and Lily – starting out with mushy food that was easy to eat, and disguising every meal as a game. With Wren and Rascal I would cut their fruit up into small chunks, then sit on the floor with them, playing games: hiding slices of apple in their favourite corners of the kitchen, or pieces of banana under the blanket from their box. Peeled grapes were particularly good, because they could kick them around the kitchen floor like they were miniature footballs and practise their 'hunting' skills. To begin with they seemed confused when the 'balls' rolled away from them, always just out of reach, but before long they'd got the hang of pinning their prey down.

They were soon happy to scamper around the kitchen when the whole family was there – except for Willow, Amber, Tarka and Blue, who were still banished to other parts of the house whenever Wren and Rascal were loose. We'd sit at the kitchen table, eating our dinner, with the quiet scratch of their claws on the floor and their little squeaks accompanying our chat. Occasionally one of us would feel a little tug at our ankle, and look down to see one of the babies trying to climb our legs. I turned a blind eye to the bits of veg that somehow made their way from the children's plates into the meerkats' mouths.

One night when we were having dinner, the

meerkats' peep-peep noises were joined by another, louder sound: Amber and Willow scratching and whimpering at the door. Lily sighed, 'Can't we let them in, Mum? It seems so unfair that they can't come into the kitchen when Wren and Rascal are out. I'm sure they won't hurt them.' I looked at Andrew; I'd been thinking the same thing. The dogs were a part of the family, and it wasn't the same without them in the kitchen, napping in their baskets, or sitting at our sides during dinner, imploring us with their soppy brown eyes to give them a scrap from the table. It was different with the cats – they were always out and about, doing whatever it is that cats do – but it felt cruel to exclude Willow and Amber from family life.

'What do you think?' I asked. He was silent for a moment, thinking. Lily and Jake looked on hopefully.

'I think if we're going to keep the meerkats in the house for the next few months, we can't go on shutting the dogs out of the room every time they're loose,' he said. 'They're good dogs, and I reckon if we handle things carefully, it should be fine.'

Later that evening, we brought Willow and Amber

into the kitchen and settled them in their baskets. I sat down on the floor next to them, stroking their fur and ready to pounce on them at a moment's notice. Andrew was similarly poised on the other side of the basket. Jake lifted Wren and Rascal's box onto the ground and picked them both up.

'Where shall I put them, Mum?' he asked.

'Over the other side of the kitchen from the dogs I think,' I said. 'Let's give them some space.'

Jake carefully placed Wren and Rascal on the floor by the kitchen table and let them go. They were immediately alert, sensing the dogs' presence. They stood up on their hind legs, sniffing the air and chattering to each other. Willow heard the noise and raised her sleepy head to see what was going on. She, too, sniffed the air.

'Dad ...?' Lily looked worried, and moved towards the meerkats, as if to pick them up and swiftly return them to the safety of the box.

'Give them a minute,' Andrew replied, looking much calmer than I felt.

I watched Willow and Amber carefully. They didn't seem too concerned about the commotion on the other side of the room. Wren and Rascal stayed upright for a few seconds, and then Rascal's attention was caught by the grape that Lily had placed on the floor, just in front of them. He said something to Wren, and together they crept forward to investigate. Amber seemed to be happily snoozing, while Willow watched the babies with apparent disinterest. I was still ready to move like lightning if she changed her mind. The meerkats made short work of the grape, and now they were more relaxed they started to move away from the box ... towards the dogs. Slowly but surely they edged forwards, curiosity obviously getting the better of them. Maybe it was because I was sitting so close to Willow and Amber, and they knew they could trust me, but they seemed fearless in their approach. Willow gave a low growl as they got closer, but remained still. The noise woke Amber, who raised her head to see what was going on. I swear I saw a flash of surprise in her eyes when she noticed the two tiny creatures boldly approaching her basket. I laid an arm over both of their backs, and murmured calming words, hoping they wouldn't suddenly leap out of the basket.

'Mum!' Lily exclaimed under her breath. 'Look how close they are now! I think it's going to be OK.'

Sure enough, Wren and Rascal were now only a few feet away from the dogs' basket. I held my breath. Still Willow and Amber did not move. I couldn't imagine that the meerkats would dare to venture any closer, but Rascal – true to form – continued his approach. I felt Willow and Amber's breathing quicken as he came right up to the basket; Wren was still hanging back, happy to let his brother take the lead.

I glanced at Andrew. I could tell he was as nervous as I was, but was trying to put on a calm facade for the benefit of the kids. Lily and Jake were crouched on the other side of the room, watching the scene unfold with rapt attention.

This was it. Rascal took one more step – mere inches now from Willow's nose – and stood up on his hind legs. He was all of six inches tall; Willow could have knocked him over with one swipe of her paw. He let out a little burst of meerkat chatter – a greeting perhaps? – and nudged her nose with his. Everyone froze. Even Wren.

Amber looked at Willow. Willow looked at Amber.

Who is this disrespectful little scamp? Should we teach him a lesson? We could ... [sigh] ... but then we'd have to get up. Amber yawned and laid her head down on her paws. Willow gave Rascal her scariest glare – which isn't very scary at all – then turned her head away from him and did the same.

I let out a huge breath I didn't even know I was still holding. Rascal, bemused that his gesture of friendship had apparently been rebuffed, turned and headed back towards the box, Wren trotting obediently behind him. Jake gathered them both up and quickly deposited them safely back in their home. Once the lid was securely fastened, we all started to laugh with relief. In the first round of meerkats vs dogs, it was honours even!

We repeated the experiment a few more times over the next few evenings, each time with the same result – although Wren and Rascal were both now practically skipping up to the basket in their eagerness to play with Amber and Willow. Once we were sure that they were all comfortable with each other, we sat back and let the dogs get out of their basket while the meerkats were loose. Again, we were poised to intervene should anyone start to get a bit too aggressive, but I'm happy to say that we never needed to. Willow and Amber are big softies at heart, and although they were certainly confused and sometimes a little irritated by these scampering creatures running all over their kitchen, they never once showed any sign of harming them. Before long, they were all rubbing along like old friends, and Wren and Rascal would use the dogs as their own personal climbing frames, clambering on their backs as they lay in their basket and using the vantage point to scan for approaching danger.

The only possible threat at this point came in the shape of our cats, who were more unpredictable – and faster – than Amber and Willow. Again, we introduced them to Wren and Rascal very slowly and not without a degree of trepidation. Blue and Tarka were definitely ... interested ... in these little mouse-like creatures. They're country cats after all, and spend many happy hours in the barn catching rats and mice. Somehow, though, they seemed instinctively to know that Wren and Rascal were off limits, and left them alone. Perhaps it was because they saw the dogs ignoring them and decided to do the same. Who knows? Of course, Wren and Rascal didn't pay them the same respect, and were constantly pushing their luck, racing around Tarka's legs, or chasing Blue's tail. Even this impertinence didn't provoke the cats into an attack though. They simply walked haughtily away, as if they had much better things to do then bother with these insignificant little mites.

Once Wren and Rascal had been successfully introduced to the whole family, we gave them the run of the downstairs for several hours a day. They were now coming up to two months old and were so lively it didn't seem fair to keep them cooped up in their box. They hardly slept at all during the day, and were always running around, playing with each other and 'foraging' for food in the kitchen. I had to keep a steady supply of fruit scattered around on the floor to stop them trying to dig up the grouting and burrow their way to Australia. And they would now sit with us in the evenings, while we watched television. We couldn't persuade them to sit on our laps – not because they were nervous of us, they simply didn't 'sit' anywhere for very long – but they would run around the living room, climbing on the furniture and rolling around on the carpet to their hearts' content. They were always together, never more than a few inches apart, and they would play-fight constantly, tumbling around together and nipping each other playfully. Tim assured us that it was all part of natural meerkat behaviour.

One night, the whole family was gathered in the living room, watching TV together. I was sitting on one sofa, cuddled up with Lily; Jake and Andrew were on the other couch, and Amber was resting her head on Andrew's lap. Willow lay stretched out in front of me and Lily, and every once in a while I reached out my foot to scratch her belly. Tarka and Blue were observing us all from the window sill, where they could also keep an eye on the goings on outside. The only movement came from Wren and Rascal, who were racing around, fully immersed in what appeared to be a game of tag. Everything was peaceful. When the advert break came on, I got up to make cups of tea and hot chocolate. As I headed out towards the kitchen, I heard Lily squeal.

'Mum, look!'

I turned around. Wren and Rascal were right behind me, standing upright and looking up at me expectantly. I looked at Lily, wondering what it was about this that had caused her to exclaim so loudly.

'They followed you, Mum! As soon as you got up to leave, they stopped playing and followed you out!'

'Do it again!' said Jake, excitedly. Obediently, I sat back down for a few seconds, and saw Wren and Rascal resume their games. Then, casually, I got up and sauntered over to the door, watching them all the while. Sure enough, they immediately stopped play-ing – mid-wrestling match – and ran over to my heels. I walked a few steps forward. They followed. I walked back into the living room; my shadows were right behind me. Jake and Lily whooped with delight.

'They think you're their mum!' Jake exclaimed. 'That must be it.'

I shook my head in amazement, not quite able to believe that the meerkat babies really thought I was their mother. I headed into the kitchen, for real this time, and switched on the kettle. I turned around and leant against the counter while I waited for it to boil. And there were my two babies, staring up at me. I smiled, and crouched down to stroke them.

'So, you think I'm Mummy Meerkat, do you?'

Wren barked softly in response, and Rascal nuzzled my hand. I felt my heart swell. These lovely little animals, who I had tended to since the day they were born, loved me as much as I loved them. I couldn't have been happier.

A Long Way from the Kalahari

'GOOOOOOAAAAL!'

Jake skidded on his knees across the lawn, cele-
brating the goal he'd just scored against his most
fearsome rivals. His opponents were definitely a force
to be reckoned with: quick, good ball skills, excellent
team work, with a nippy little duo up front. Not so
good in defence though ...

'Nice one, Jake!' I shouted from the decking, where
I was carrying out a number of important roles:
crowd, scorekeeper, referee (I'd already had to get out
my yellow card a few times), physio and refreshments
lady. 'I make that Collier FC 2 – Meerkats Utd 0. And
there's only five minutes left before fulltime.'

With that Jake tore off after the ball, Wren and

Rascal hot on his heels. Ever since we'd discovered they had a liking for football – Jake's number one pastime – I often found the three of them racing around the garden. The ball dwarfed the meerkats, but they didn't seem intimidated by its size and loved chasing it all over the garden. My floral borders were taking a bit of a battering, but they were all having so much fun that I didn't have the heart to scold. A few minutes later I called both teams into the kitchen for orange slices – a refreshing snack they could all enjoy!

Wren and Rascal were now ten weeks old, and seemed to be getting bigger by the day. They looked exactly like adult meerkats – with the distinctive black rings around their eyes, striped bodies and long, curling tails – but they were still a good bit smaller than their fully grown relatives up at the park. They continued to sleep in their box in the kitchen, but as long as there was someone in the house, they ran loose most of the time. We'd started letting them out into the garden a few weeks ago, and watching them explore the lawn and flower beds – which must have seemed like paradise after spending two months in the house – was a real delight. By now, nothing seemed to faze them; there was none of the timidity I'd witnessed when they took their first steps out of their box and into the kitchen. They charged around the garden, investigating every last centimetre, their little noses twitching away as they took in all of the new smells. They loved it. It was already spring and we spent every spare second outside, watching the meerkats play with each other on the lawn.

But it wasn't all plain sailing for Wren and Rascal. One day the three of us were out in the garden: I was doing some weeding in one of my football-battered flower beds, and the meerkats were sunning themselves on the decking of our house. Meerkats have 'solar panels' on their tummies, and love nothing more than stretching out in the sunshine to recharge their batteries. I was absorbed in my task – trying to decide if a flattened pansy could be rescued – and content to let them sunbathe in peace. I knew they wouldn't wander off. Suddenly, the tranquillity was interrupted by an almighty squawk and a burst of alarmed barking from Wren and Rascal. I jumped up, turning towards the house. There, bold as brass, was our peacock – who usually lives up at the park – standing proudly in front of the decking, all his colourful feathers on flamboyant display. He was screeching loudly. I quickly looked for Wren and Rascal, and just caught sight of their tails disappearing into the house at great speed. I ran in after them, heading straight for the kitchen, which has always been their first refuge when they feel frightened. Sure enough, there they were, standing upright on the far side of the room – as far away from that strange beast as they could manage – chattering to each other loudly. Poor things – they were terrified! I hurried towards them, and they quickly scurried over to my ankles, seeking comfort. I picked them both up and gave them a big cuddle; I could feel their little hearts racing. I held them up to my face, looking into their anxious little eyes.

'Oh, you poor things,' I soothed, 'what a fright!' Wren gave a little squeak in response, nuzzling my hand with his nose. I'd never seen them look so scared before – they had been so sheltered here at the house, and hadn't yet encountered any of the park's weird and wonderful creatures. They were now as used to Willow, Amber, Blue and Tarka as they were to Jake and Lily, and just considered them to be a normal part of their lives. I put them both down in their box, where they burrowed under their blanket, taking refuge just like a wild meerkat would in an underground tunnel.

I sat down with a heavy sigh, concerned that they'd had such a scare. In the back of my mind I knew that we'd soon have to think about moving Wren and Rascal up to the park, but how would they cope away from the home comforts of the farmhouse? Was it fair to expect them to adjust to the new environment in the same way that our other animals did? New arrivals always took a while to settle in, but they usually came to us from another park or zoo, or in many cases were born and bred at Axe Valley. They were used to being surrounded by other animals and humans. If Wren and Rascal were that frightened of the peacock, I could only imagine what they'd make of Ringo! Perhaps we needed to expose them gradually to the animals who would be their new neighbours, and try to get them acclimatised. I must admit the idea of the babies – I still thought of them that way – moving up to the park made me sad. They wouldn't be far away, I knew that, but I'd got so used to having them with me nearly all the time that it wrenched at my heart to know they'd soon be independent adults who wouldn't rely on me nearly as much. What if they stopped coming to me for cuddles? I shook my head, laughing at myself – if I was getting this depressed at the thought of Wren and Rascal moving a few hundred yards away, what on earth would I be like when Lily and Jake left home?

That night I told Andrew about Wren and Rascal's peacock encounter, and for the first time we discussed the possibility of them moving up to the park. We agreed that it was time to start building them an enclosure of their own – they couldn't be housed with Mango and Tango and they'd need plenty of room to run around. Andrew could tell I was worried about letting them go, and suggested that to begin with we could have them at the park during the day and then

Me with Wren and Rascal. Wren is on my back, acting as lookout.

The three meerkat babies snuggled up on the Aga. At this point I wasn't sure if they would survive and just wanted to get them warmed up as soon as possible. Sadly, the third baby died shortly afterwards.

Wren and Rascal aged about four weeks old.

Wren and Rascal use me as a climbing frame.

Rascal in a staring competition with Tarka.

Jake teaches Wren and Rascal how to play cricket.

What's this then? Wren and Rascal investigate Richard Austin's camera.

Rascal gets his own back on
the peacock.

Let's hope meerkats don't get
hay fever.

Wren and a host of
golden daffodils.

My nemesis: Ringo.

Ringo takes on the dustbin lid.

A familiar routine: hand-feeding Zorro, the baby coati.

Andrew tempts RJ with a bit of hot cross bun. Mind your fingers!

Lily models this year's most fashionable head gear: the coati.

Home sweet home.

bring them back to the house at night. And while their new enclosure was being constructed, we could start gently introducing them to some of our more exotic friends.

I felt better with a plan in place, and went to bed that night somewhat reassured that everything would work out OK. Wren and Rascal seemed to have forgotten about their big fright, and had spent the evening happily playing with Jake and Lily. Tomorrow, we'd scout out a plot for their new home and I had grand plans to begin their animal-education programme!

Before long, Wren and Rascal's enclosure began to take shape. Andrew, Jake and my dad, Alan, had had lots of fun plotting it all out and then constructing a fantastic little pied-à-terre for our favourite meerkats. It wouldn't be long before it was time to move them in.

In the meantime, I'd been figuring out how best to prepare them. I decided that before we took them up to the park, they should meet an animal that was as gentle as it was big: the cow. So one lovely summer's evening, after the park was closed, I led my little troupe on an exciting expedition up to the farm. We must have made quite a comical sight: me, Andrew, Jake, Lily, Amber, Willow, Wren and Rascal, progressing slowly up the lane towards the field where the herd was grazing. We went very, *very*, slowly. The meerkats stopped every few feet to sniff at the hedgerows, delighted to have new territories to explore. Occasionally they'd disappear for a moment, but they always popped up again a few seconds later, often with leaves and twigs attached to them. We all stopped and laughed as Rascal struggled to shake a stubborn bit of hawthorn off his head. 'You're a long way from the Kalahari, aren't you, Rascal?' joked Andrew, bending down to remove the offending piece of hedge.

'And there are definitely no evil peacocks in the desert!' laughed Jake, still amused by the meerkats' feathery encounter.

'Aw, poor Wren and Rascal!' Lily playfully shoved her brother. 'How would you like it if you were screeched at by a bird ten times bigger than you?'

'Hardly *ten* times,' said Jake, 'but I suppose you're right. Imagine a giant blue and green bird appearing out of nowhere! That's definitely enough to scare anyone.'

Willow and Amber found our leisurely progress frustrating; they kept racing ahead, then noticing that we weren't keeping up and circling back to encourage us to get a move on. But we eventually arrived at our destination, only a few hundred yards from the house. We stood at the gate, looking out into the field where the herd were happily munching on grass or snoozing. Wren and Rascal were still charging about, investigating everything around them and apparently oblivious to the giant beasts in the neighbouring field. I called them and they dashed over to our feet. I doubted they could see much from their vertically-challenged vantage point, so I picked them up and, holding them in one hand, pointed to the cows in the field. 'Wren, Rascal ... I'd like to introduce you to our cows. They're the biggest animals we own. If you can make friends with these guys, I reckon you'll be fine up at the park.' They didn't seem interested.

Eventually one of the herd noticed us and wandered over to the gate to see what was going on. This got the meerkats' attention, and their little noses started to twitch nervously. Rascal let out a little 'eek!' of alarm, and Lily giggled. I kept a tight hold on them both, suddenly anxious that they might struggle out of my grip and make a run for it if they got too scared. After a few moments, though, I could sense them start to relax. I don't think the cow had really registered their presence and in any case she wasn't paying them any attention. Wren and Rascal now seemed more intrigued than alarmed, and I realised the real danger wasn't of them running away, but running *towards* the cows, who probably seemed to them like bigger versions of their friends Amber and Willow. Imagine climbing up on the back of one of these fellows – the views would be fantastic! Judging our first experiment a success – or perhaps deciding to quit while we were ahead – we began the slow walk home. I felt reassured that Wren and Rascal were growing up to be confident little chaps, and although there were sure to be a few anxious moments when we took them up to the park for the first time, I knew they could handle anything. Apart from peacocks, that is.

Before I knew it, the big day arrived. I must admit that I didn't get much sleep the night before. I wasn't nervous anymore about how the meerkats would cope ... it was *me* I was worried about. I'd become so attached to them, and so used to organising my life around their routine, that I couldn't imagine what my day would be like with them living independently at the park.

The plan was simple. We'd do the usual morning feeds and open up the park, then put the finishing touches to the enclosure – laying the bark and hiding lots of lovely fruit in the various nooks and crannies as a housewarming present for Wren and Rascal – and then we'd all accompany the meerkats up to their new home. While all this last-minute preparatory work was taking place, Lily and Jake, who were both on half-term, would look after the meerkats at the house.

Their new home was really lovely. It wasn't as big as Mango and Tango's palatial enclosure, but as they were still quite small and there were only two of them, they didn't need quite as much space. And I still hoped we'd be able to let them out to run around at regular intervals. It had mesh sides, so that we'd be able to watch everything they go up to, and no 'roof', so that they could see out and we could see in – and reach in to give them cuddles! Andrew had laid various plastic pipes for them to run around in, and piled up some logs for them to climb on. The floor was made of chicken wire covered in a lovely thick layer of bark. (The chicken wire was to stop them attempting a Great Escape.) It was a perfect little starter home; the equivalent of a studio flat. In time we'd have to build them something bigger, but this was just right for getting them used to the park. And as they'd be coming inside at night, there was no need for them to have any sleeping quarters in the enclosure, which gave them all the more room for playing.

I finished spreading out the bark, made sure there was fresh water in their bowl, and then climbed out. The enclosure was ready for its new inhabitants. I called out to Andrew, who was over by one of the aviaries, repairing a gate's broken latch. Together we headed home to collect Wren and Rascal and the children. As we approached the house, I could see Lily waiting for us, hopping about in excitement. But, hang on a minute ... she didn't *look* excited. She looked worried. I realised she was actually jiggling from one foot to the other with anxiety.

'Lily, what is it?' I asked, immediately concerned.

'Um ...' she looked reluctant to tell me.

'It's OK, sweetie,' I reassured her. 'You can tell us.'

'It's Wren!' she blurted out. 'We can't find him!'

We immediately ran into the house, where Jake was sitting at the table with a forlorn-looking Rascal in his arms. I felt a deep sense of dread; after all we'd been through with the meerkats, what if we lost one today, on what was supposed to be a day of celebration? I couldn't bear to think about it.

'What happened?' Andrew asked, anxiously.

Jake took a deep breath and explained. He was clearly very upset. 'We'd been playing with them in the living room, but then Lil went to make them some lunch and I went to get something from my room – just for a second! – and when I got back they'd run off. You know, like they do ...' I nodded, and put my arm round his shoulders. 'I found Rascal upstairs in the bathroom, but we can't find Wren anywhere.'

'It's OK,' I looked at them both; they were clearly

worried they'd be in trouble. 'It's not your fault. You can't watch them both every second, and they're so quick they can disappear before you've even blinked. I'm surprised we haven't lost one before.'

Andrew nodded. 'I'm sure Wren is fine, but we'd better try and find him fast before he gets into too much trouble. Where have you looked?'

Lily, looking a little less anxious, told us they'd searched every room and done a circuit of the house to check Wren hadn't escaped outside. We put Rascal in his box – he looked so lonely, he'd never been apart from his brother for this long before – and went off to do another thorough search. Despite reassuring the children that Wren was sure to be OK, I was defi- nitely worried. I'd spent enough time with the meerkats to know they could move very quickly, and dig their way into all sorts of tricky spots. We split up: Jake and I searching upstairs; Andrew and Lily down- stairs. We started out in Jake's room, where there were hundreds of places for an enterprising meerkat to hide. We looked under all of the furniture, locating in the process several missing socks and a football boot that we had given up for lost. We pulled the wardrobe away from the wall to see if Wren was hiding behind it. I stood on a chair and looked on top of the wardrobe, and on the highest shelves of Jake's bookcase, knowing that Wren would be able to climb up anything if he put his mind to it. Nothing. Lily's room next: again, nothing.

On our way to the bathroom I shouted downstairs, asking Andrew if they'd found any signs of Wren down there. Lily appeared at the bottom of the stairs; she looked on the verge of tears.

'No, we can't find him anywhere. What if he's trapped or hurt somewhere?'

Similar thoughts had been racing through my mind, but I smiled at my kind, gentle daughter and reassured her that Wren was simply good at hide and seek, and that even if we didn't find him ourselves, he'd definitely reappear when he was hungry.

'Mum!' Jake shouted to me from the bathroom. 'Come in here quickly! I think I can hear him!' I beckoned to Lily and she ran up the stairs, Andrew right behind her. We all piled into the bathroom to find Jake crouched down with his ear pressed against the bath panelling.

'I think he's *inside* the bath,' Jake said in amazement. 'I can hear him scrabbling around in there!'

Andrew quickly knelt down next to him and adopted the same odd position, a look of intense concentration on his face. Suddenly, he smiled. 'He's right! There's definitely something in there.'

'How did he get in?' Lily wondered. I scanned the panelling which stretched all around the bathtub and quickly located a hole that wasn't usually there. Wren must have burrowed his way inside. And of course, there was little hope of him coming out the way he'd gotten in. With a sigh of resignation, Andrew went to fetch his tools, and one by one, removed the tongue-and-groove panels he'd spent ages putting up only a few years earlier. Once there was a decent, head-sized gap, I peered in and sure enough there was Wren, right in the far corner, out of reach. He didn't look hurt, and when I called his name he showed no interest in coming out at all. He didn't even react when we brought some mealworms up and waved them temptingly in front of him. He was obviously enjoying himself. Andrew removed another couple of panels to allow us to reach in further. This time I thought I'd just be able to grab him if I wriggled under the bath a bit myself. But wouldn't you know it, just as I was manoeuvring myself into position, Wren decided to saunter out of his own accord, dusty but no worse for wear.

Lily quickly picked him up, giving him a big hug and a kiss on the head. The little scallywag looked completely unconcerned with the chaos he'd caused, and simply basked in the attention. We took him downstairs to reunite him with his brother, who chattered in excitement when he saw Wren being lowered into the box. Everyone collapsed onto nearby chairs, exhausted by all the drama.

'Right then, shall we take these wretched creatures up to the park,' asked Andrew, with a smile, 'before they get into any more trouble here?'

Celebrities

Wren and Rascal had been living in the park for a few weeks and so far the whole enterprise had been a huge success. They loved their enclosure, and never seemed to tire of exploring all its various crevices. I enjoyed getting back into my usual routine of spending all day at the park – rather than being tied to the house – and I could stop by Wren and Rascal's pen as often as I wanted. They still greeted me with great enthusiasm, and it was a real treat to be able to break off from mucking out or cutting up frozen chicks to go and sit with them for a cuddle. After we'd closed up the park for the day, I'd head back to the house with my two meerkat shadows scampering along at my heels.

From day one, they were a real hit with our visitors. Mango and Tango had long been one of our most popular attractions, but the fact that Wren and Rascal were so tame was a real added bonus. We didn't let anyone else handle them (I was sure they wouldn't hurt anyone, but imagine if they did!) but everyone enjoyed watching them climb all over me whenever I sat with them in their pen. I was sitting there one day, feeding grapes to Rascal while Wren clambered up my leg, being watched by a little boy of about three and his mum. He was enthralled by the meerkats, and kept tugging at his mum's sleeve.

'Simples! Simples, Mummy! It's simples.'

'Yes, sweetie. Well done! Aren't you clever?'

'Simples! Simples! Simples!' he repeated, jumping up and down and pointing at Rascal.

'Good boy!' she said, smiling proudly, and then pulled him away to look at the lemurs in the next enclosure. As they walked away, I could hear him still insistently saying 'simples' to her, and craning his head to look back at Wren and Rascal. He was obviously *really* keen on that word.

'What was that about?' I asked Rascal, who was sitting on my knee and attacking another grape. He looked up at me for a moment, as if to say, 'What are you wittering on about? I'm *trying* to eat my lunch.' I shrugged and got up to leave them to their food, heading off to prepare a snack for RJ. I'd soon forgotten all about it.

❋

'Rascal, *no!* . . . I'm sorry, go on.'

'I'm a wildlife photographer,' said the voice at the other end of phone, 'and I was wondering if . . .'

'RASCAL! Excuse me one moment, would you?' Rascal was climbing the curtains, swinging perilously several feet off the ground. I put down the phone and dashed over to the window, disentangling the mischievous meerkat and placing him in his box, where he couldn't get into any trouble. I ran back to the phone again.

'I'm so sorry,' I gasped. 'I'm having trouble with my . . . cat. What were you saying?'

'I'm a wildlife photographer,' he repeated, patiently. 'I was wondering if I could come up to your park and take some photographs.'

'Oh! Um, well, I'm sure that would be fine,' I replied, somewhat taken aback by his request. Didn't wildlife photographers usually spend their time staking out lions on the Masai Mara? As if sensing my slight confusion, he jumped in quickly to explain.

'I live locally, and it's such a fantastic opportunity to have all these wonderful animals close by. Sometimes I can spend days waiting to get a shot of an animal in the wild, but with you I hope I'd be able to get loads of great pictures without all the hanging about. And the papers often take my pictures, so there could be some publicity in it for you.'

Well, that was enough to persuade me. I told him about the animals we had and we arranged a time for his visit. As I put the phone down, Andrew wandered into the kitchen and I filled him in on the phone call. I was excited about the possibility of some of our animals being featured in the newspaper – just imagine the publicity that could give the park. Andrew – always the pragmatist in our relationship – warned me not to get my hopes up. But I had a good feeling about this.

About a week before the photographer – Richard Austin – was due to visit, I was walking past the meerkats' pen when I noticed a group of children, around Jake's age, leaning over the fence watching Wren and Rascal. I had just stopped to make sure they weren't about to dangle any fingers over the edge when I heard one of them say 'simples'. That word again! I walked over to join them.

'They're *so* cool!' one of the boys exclaimed. 'Just like the one on TV.'

'Yeah, all they need is one of those funny tie things,' his friend said, laughing.

'A cravat,' the lone girl in the group added, wisely. 'It's called a cravat.'

Now I was really confused – meerkats in cravats? 'Hello,' I said, joining them at the fence. 'Who wears a cravat?'

They looked embarrassed, and I could tell they were on the verge of clamming up after being interrupted by a grown-up. 'Sorry,' I backtracked. 'I'm only being nosy, you don't have to tell me ... I work here, by the way – those are my meerkats.'

'Really?' said the girl, her eyes wide. 'They're awesome!'

I smiled. 'They are, aren't they?' I looked down

into the pen and noticed Wren and Rascal both standing upright in their best 'I'm a wild meerkat' poses; showing off for the crowd. I told the group all about hand-rearing them, and the adventures we'd had together. They all looked suitably impressed.

'I guess you get a lot of people mentioning those adverts?' one of the boys said, shyly. Now we were getting somewhere.

'Which adverts?' They all looked at each other in amazement. Obviously I'd said something especially uncool.

'*You* know,' the girl said, in exactly the same tone of voice Lily uses when she's particularly exasperated with me. 'The ones all over telly, with the Russian meerkat … the one with the funny voice who's always saying "simples".'

I was still none the wiser. 'Sorry, never seen them,' I admitted.

'Oh miss, you got to,' she said. (Miss! As if I was one of their teachers!) 'They're wicked. You can watch them on YouTube I reckon.'

And with that piece of advice – as if I ever had the

time to go on YouTube – an adult voice called them away and off they ran, shouting 'Bye, miss!' as they went. I resolved to ask Jake to find this famous advert online. Apparently I was the only person in the world who hadn't seen it.

It all became clear that evening when Jake showed me the clip. It featured a Russian meerkat – complete with smoking jacket and, yes, a cravat – who advertised an online price-comparison site. 'Simples' was his catchphrase. I shook my head in disbelief: what would they think of next? I had to admit he was funny, but I still thought Wren and Rascal were the cutest meerkats around. Over the next few days we noticed that the 'simples' phenomenon seemed to escalate. I would hear a child (and sometimes an adult) excitedly quoting the famous meerkat's motto a few times a day, and there was always a notable crowd around both meerkat enclosures. It seemed unbelievable that one little advert could be having this effect, but if it brought more people to the park then I wasn't going to complain!

'Are you ready for your close-up, Rascal?' I asked the little meerkat, as he clambered onto my knee in an attempt to reach the dog biscuit in my hand. Today was the day of the big photoshoot, and I had stopped by Wren and Rascal's enclosure to feed them their breakfast and make sure they were looking present-able. I picked a sliver of bark out of Rascal's fur and wondered which animals Richard would choose to photograph. He hadn't said on the phone – he just wanted to look around the park and see what took his fancy. I really hoped he would pick Wren and Rascal – I just knew they'd be brilliant little models and it would be really special to have some nice pic-tures of them as mementoes of our adventures together.

A few hours later I was showing Richard around the park, introducing him to all the animals. Sometimes it's only when I'm giving someone new the guided tour that I realise how much we've achieved here. You can easily become blind to the things you see every day, so it's a great feeling to look at the park through somebody else's eyes. Today, when visitors drive up to Axe Valley Bird and Animal

Park, they see a beautiful, hand-painted wooden sign, welcoming them to what we hope will be a place they'll want to come back to again and again, somewhere different than the usual zoo or wildlife park. They leave their cars in the small parking area, and enter by a gate where we take their entrance fee and they can pick up some information sheets about the animals inside. Once they're in the park, they can follow the various paths any way round they want to – there's no set route. It would only take about ten minutes to walk around the whole place if you didn't stop to look at anything, but most visitors stay for at least an hour – sometimes much longer. The paths meander around the enclosures and I've planted shrubs and flowers along each route, which makes everything look really pretty and I hope reminds people that this is an extension of our home, not just another zoo. There are tables where families can eat their own picnics, a kiosk where we sell teas, coffees and Mum's homemade cakes and there's even a swing-set and seesaw for kids. We have various chickens and the peacocks wandering around freely and there are pens with guinea pigs and rabbits that children can pick up and cuddle. I could tell Richard was impressed when I told him about how we'd started out with an empty paddock and how we still had plans to expand and improve.

'This is amazing!' he said. 'I can't believe this is all right here on my doorstep . . . it's such a little treasure trove.'

I was delighted. Richard had seen thousands of animals in the wild and visited many big famous wildlife parks, so it was a real thrill to hear him speak so warmly of our little menagerie. But there was still one thing I was desperate for him to see. He had been really enthusiastic about all the animals I'd shown him, but he hadn't said for sure which ones he wanted to photograph. By this point we had been walking around the park for twenty minutes and I had deliberately left Wren and Rascal's enclosure until last. As we approached, I could see Wren on top of the biggest log in their pen, peering out around the park. Because the fences to their enclosure are quite low, compared to those of the other animals in the park, you can often see their little heads popping up to check out what's going on or who is approaching.

When Wren saw it was me, he shouted to Rascal and they ran over to the fence to meet me.

'And this,' I said, proudly, 'is the home of some of our most recent additions, Wren and Rascal. Hand-reared meerkats.'

Richard turned to me, obviously surprised. 'Hand-reared?' he exclaimed. 'That's incredible. I've never heard of anyone doing that before. What happened?'

I quickly filled him in on the past nine months' adventures, as I climbed into the enclosure and sat down on a log. Wren and Rascal both immediately climbed onto my knee. Richard looked delighted.

'Do you still let them out?' he asked, hopefully.

'Oh yes,' I replied. 'They still come back inside every night and they'll run around the house and garden quite safely. They tend to follow me wherever I go, so as long as that's not walking down a busy street, I'm happy to let them out pretty much anywhere now.'

He eyes lit up. 'Well then, I think I've found today's stars. Would you mind if I took some photos of them in various different locations? I'm sure I'd be able to sell their pictures. Everyone *loves* meerkats – especially at the moment.'

I nodded, glad I knew now that he was referring to the famous television meerkat. 'Of course. Wren and Rascal ... Rascal in particular, in fact ... are both real show-offs and I know you'll have no trouble getting them to strike a pose or two.'

Turns out I was right. Richard ended up staying for four hours and took hundreds and hundreds of pictures. Wren and Rascal absolutely loved all the attention, and behaved impeccably – no diva-like attitudes from my little supermodels. They were photographed in the garden, playing with (or should I say, attacking) a colourful peacock's feather and a lovely yellow sunflower – I think they were pleased to get revenge on the peacock! Richard also snapped them playing cricket with Jake and climbing all over his spare camera, investigating the strange contraption that kept being pointed in their direction. He even took some pictures of them with me (which I was not prepared for) and had the three of us in all sorts of positions – including me lying on my front with my head propped up in my hands and Wren and Rascal standing alert on my back. I couldn't imagine anyone would want those pictures. The ones I was most looking forward to seeing, though, were a whole series Richard took of both meerkats in a beautiful field of daffodils not far from the farm. They weren't much taller than the flowers themselves, and they looked so gorgeous standing there in the middle of a real 'host' of golden flowers. Wren even stuck his little head inside the trumpet of one of the flowers at one point – I really hoped that Richard had managed to get a snap of that.

When Richard drove away, after telling me that he'd send the pictures on a disk in the next few days, I walked Wren and Rascal back to their enclosure and gave them an extra big bowl of food as a reward for all their hard work. Even if no one else ever wanted to see the pictures, at least I knew we'd have some really lovely keepsakes to treasure.

The pictures Richard sent through were as fantastic as I'd hoped they would be – even the ones with me in weren't too bad. And he had managed to capture Wren with his head inside the daffodil's trumpet, looking for all the world as if he was smelling its scent. Richard said his agent would start sending them around to the press agencies, and that's when a newspaper might pick one to fill a gap on one of their pages. I resolved not to get too excited about that possibility and instead concentrated on every-day life at Summer Farm. We might have had two almost-famous meerkats in our midst, but life still went on as usual and every day on the farm is busy and filled with things to do from dawn until dusk.

Lily is really into horseriding, just like I was when I was younger, and she is lucky enough to be being trained in dressage by a wonderful woman named Vicky, who used to ride professionally (she even rode in front of the Queen!) and has taken Lily under her wing. Lily is incredibly dedicated and rides Vicky's horses – Pickle and Delfi – every night. She has already ridden in a few one-day events, doing dressage and cross-country, and her ambition is to one day ride at Badminton Horse Trials. I've no doubt that she'll make it there. I must admit that my heart is always in my mouth when we watch her, at least to begin with, and I can barely look as she goes flying over the jumps, but she's completely

fearless and after a while her enthusiasm becomes con-
tagious and I start to relax and enjoy it. If I'm not taking
Lily to the stables, then chances are I'm ferrying Jake
to football practice or a game. He plays for the Colyton
under-13s and they practise on Wednesday nights
and play every Saturday morning – we all try to be there
to watch him and cheer the team on if we can, and
I help out the manager with emails to the team and
collecting fees on match days. I'm a huge football fan –
I inherited a passion for Manchester United from my
dad – so I love watching Jake play and I'd be lying if
I said I hadn't thought about him one day playing
at Old Trafford! Andrew and I are so proud of both
children, and although I have to be super organised
about remembering who needs to be where and when,
we don't begrudge them their activities for one moment.
Because of the park, we're not able to take many holidays or get away together very often, and they really
are brilliant at helping out and pulling their weight.
Andrew and I are happy that they both have hobbies
they enjoy, and we do everything we can to make sure
they're able to get as much out of them as possible.

A few days later I was pulling up to the house after performing a double-whammy in the Mum Taxi – dropping off Jake at football and Lily at the stables in one go – when I saw my own mum come dashing out of the back door, beckoning me in.

'Jayne! Phone for you ... it's that photographer.' She looked excited, and I walked quickly into the kitchen and picked up the phone, hoping Richard had some good news for us.

'Hello Richard, it's Jayne.'

'Jayne, hi! I'm glad I caught you, I was just telling your mum that I've got some exciting news.'

I was on tenterhooks. 'Yes ...?'

'The *Western Morning News* are interested in some of the pictures of Wren and Rascal, and what's more, they want to interview you!'

'Me!' I squeaked. 'Why?'

'They saw the picture of you with the meerkats and asked about the story behind it. We told them and they said they'd love to write a short feature about everything that's happened to you.'

I couldn't believe it. Wren and Rascal having their picture in the paper was one thing, but a whole interview with me ... it just seemed unreal. Nervous as I was, I agreed to do it because I knew it would be good publicity for the park. But what would I say? My palms started to sweat at the thought of being interviewed. Thankfully I didn't have much time to worry about it – Richard said the journalist would be calling me that morning, and sure enough the phone rang less than ten minutes later. I'd barely had time to fill Mum in on the details before I was chatting away to a really nice lady who asked me all sorts of questions about Wren and Rascal. I needn't have worried about what to say, she asked so many questions and seemed so interested in my answers that in the end she had trouble shutting me up. We spoke for about fifteen minutes and then she told me that the article would appear in the paper at some point over the next few weeks. I was a strange mixture of nervous and excited, and I wasn't sure I'd be able to stand the wait.

Luckily the article appeared only a few days later, and of course we bought several copies to keep as souvenirs. I sat in the car outside the newsagents in

Kilmington, rifling through the pages, eager to find
the article and see what it looked like. I couldn't
believe it when I saw we filled up half a page – they'd
included the picture of me with Wren and Rascal,
which I was a bit embarrassed about, but the article
was great and included details about the park. We
hoped people would read it and be inspired to come
and meet Wren and Rascal in the flesh. Of course,
they'd mentioned the famous Russian meerkat in the
first paragraph – there was no getting away from him
these days. I'd seen something else in the paper about
him recently, talking about how many fans he had on
the Internet and how he had starting a whole meerkat
memorabilia trend. Perhaps we should start selling
toy meerkats at the park?

The phone rang off the hook in the days after the
article appeared, with friends and family wanting to
know how the article had come about and congratu-
lating us on our moment in the spotlight. We also
noticed that visitor numbers that weekend were up –
the publicity seemed to be having the desired effect.

A few weeks after the article appeared in the *Western
Morning News*, there was even more excitement. A

national newspaper had picked up on the story and wanted to run a feature on us. This time I really was speechless: I just couldn't believe what was happening. Everyone else in the family was jumping up and down with excitement, but I just sat there in a daze. It didn't seem possible that people could be so interested in what we were doing. In rescuing Wren and Rascal that morning, I had only done what I was sure anyone else in my position (which, granted, was an unusual one) would have done, and I suddenly felt uncomfortable being the centre of attention. I didn't want anyone to think we were seeking fame for fame's sake. All I wanted was for the stories to bring visitors to the park, so that people could enjoy the animals and we could continue to do what we loved. For that reason I agreed to do the interview, but as I walked over to the park that afternoon to greet a visitor, I couldn't help but wonder what those little meerkats had got us into this time.

My Family and Other Animals

I wouldn't blame anyone for thinking that Wren and Rascal were the only animals we had to take care of at Axe Valley, or the only ones who got up to any mischief. The young meerkats certainly kept us busy, but we had hundreds of other animals and birds to look after, too, and they all worked equally hard to keep us entertained and on our toes. From the first day I found Wren and Rascal to the moment their photos appeared in the paper, life in the park had carried on as usual. And of course, 'usual' for us nearly always meant *un*usual! There were new arrivals to the park (two hand-reared female deer – one fallow and one red – who both needed bottle-feeding twice a day), new babies (skunks ... yes, they require very careful handling), new homes (for the agoutis – relatives of the guinea pig) and always something new for us to learn, repair or build. There were also one or two unexpected surprises.

I remember one day, when Wren and Rascal were only a few months old, I was doing some washing up in the kitchen after lunch and wondering if I had time to let the babies out for a run around before I went back up to the park. When Andrew walked in, I thought nothing of it – he often pops back to the house for a cup of tea when it's quiet up at the park – but then I saw he was carrying a box in his hands.

'What's that? A present?' I joked, guessing it was unlikely to be chocolates.

'A baby owl,' he responded, matter-of-factly. Of course, who wouldn't carry a baby owl around in a box? Mind you, I was one to talk – I had my own baby meerkats in a box, after all. Andrew opened the flaps to show me, explaining that some work-men from the local council had been trimming unruly trees nearby when they found the tiny owl on the ground, with no mother in sight. One of them knew about the park and brought the bird straight to us, believing it was in the baby bird's best interests to get it help as soon as possible. It was a tiny thing, covered in a light, downy fluff and with its eyes still firmly closed – it couldn't have been more than a few days old. Andrew was certainly more than capable of caring for the owl but we both knew there was a good chance that if the workmen had left the baby alone for a while, they would have seen its mother find it and take it back to the nest. Now it had been handled, it could never be returned to her. If you do find a baby animal or bird in the wild, and it appears to have been abandoned, it is always best to sit back and observe for a while, to make sure that really is the case. You should only interfere as a last resort, and then take it straight to your local RSPCA or RSPB branch. But the workmen had done what they thought was best, out of kindness, and now the owl was here we would have to do our best to look after it. So, over the next few months Andrew cared for the baby owl as attentively as I looked after the meerkats, keeping up a regular feeding regime of small chunks of meat (usually chicks and mice) and making sure it was always safe and warm. That baby owl, a male named Echo, was soon as attached to Andrew as Wren and Rascal were to me. He began to fly for short distances at around two months, so Andrew would let him fly around the barn for exercise, and then eventually we started to let him out in the park. And that's where we got into trouble ...

To begin with, Echo would fly about quite happily, always returning to Andrew when he was called or when he caught the scent of the chick Andrew would use as a lure. We weren't worried about him straying too far, because he was still young and wasn't able to fly for prolonged periods. But while Echo might not have been able to fly very far, that didn't mean he couldn't get into mischief. One day, when he was about three months old, and Andrew and I were both at the park doing our regular chores, Echo managed to get stuck in the highest branch of one of our tallest trees ... and didn't come down for four hours. We were relaxed about it to begin with – thinking that he'd make his way down eventually – but as time went on and our repeated calls to him made no difference, we began to worry. He was still too young to catch his own food, and the longer he was up there, the hungrier he would get. There was also the danger – however slight it might seem – that a larger bird of prey looking for a quick snack might swoop in and snatch Echo right off the branch. We were just debating whether Andrew could scale the tree using our tallest ladder (and I was secretly considering a call to the fire brigade – after all, they rescue cats from trees, why not owls?) when Mum, who'd been patiently calling to Echo and trying to tempt him down with some meat, was finally successful. He came hurtling down out of the tree, more falling than flying – hunger obviously getting the better of whatever nerves had been keeping him up there in the first place – and landed on Andrew's arm, scratching him quite badly in the process. We were hugely relieved. Echo had been a surprise arrival at the farm – and one we weren't jumping for joy about, if I'm honest – but we'd all become really attached to the little fledgling and as with all our animals, the thought of anything bad happening to him was too awful to consider.

Echo is now eight months old and still living

happily at the park with our other owls. A happy ending, if ever I heard one.

There was one break-out attempt from the park which was rather more successful, involving our young mara. Not many people know about maras, but they're really brilliant little animals – a relative of the guinea pig, from South America, they're a sort of cross between a rabbit and a deer ... in that their faces look a little bit like deer, but they hop about like rabbits. Our mara, a relatively recent addition to the park, shares an enclosure with Ringo and the wallabies and she's a really sweet little thing. Or so we thought. It was a busy day in the park on the day she made her break for freedom. I was doing some gardening not far from her enclosure, and I'd seen her in there only moments earlier, munching on some grass. The next time I glanced up, she was nowhere to be seen. Had she hopped over the fence? Maras can jump very high, but surely she couldn't have cleared the six-foot fence? But we didn't have time to figure out how she'd done it, we needed to find her – and fast.

Andrew and I did a quick circuit of the park, taking the path in opposite directions and trying to carry out a thorough search without alarming any of the visitors – peering into all the flowerbeds and different potential hiding places. We'd soon looked everywhere but couldn't see her anywhere at all. Then I suddenly spotted her little tail bouncing down the drive and, after calling for Andrew to join me, we both ran to catch up with her. She was a wily little thing though, and every time we got close, she managed to outwit us and hop away. Before we knew it, she'd burrowed through a gap in the hedge and seemed to have completely vanished. We searched for her far and wide, each taking turns to stay at the park while the other combed the nearby fields and paths looking for her. There was still no sign of her. Jake and Lily joined the search party after school, but even with our increased numbers, we couldn't see her anywhere. Dejected, we all went home to bed, worried we'd lost her for good.

The next morning, we set out again, going over some of the same ground and extending our search area further afield. Still nothing. Then, when we'd finally given up hope, the phone rang. It was one of our neighbours.

'There's a funny-looking animal in my paddock, grazing with the sheep. Unless there's a circus in town, I think it's probably one of yours.'

We thanked him profusely and Andrew, his brother-in-law, Erik, and I jumped into the car to head for our neighbour's field as quickly as we could. We were armed with large fishing nets – the nearest thing to a mara-catcher we had at our disposal. We spotted her straight away, hopping around the paddock merrily and no doubt confusing the sheep. We crept into the field slowly, cautiously, afraid that too much noise might cause her to bolt again. But in spite of our stealth, she soon saw us, and the sprightly little thing hopped away as soon as we got near with the nets. She charged across the paddock at an amazing speed, and set off up the lane. Andrew and I ran after her, and Erik followed slowly behind in the truck. As we pounded up the lane, I realised we were heading in the direction of Vicky's house, where Lily was having her riding lesson. I pulled my mobile out of my pocket and called her, running all the while. When she answered, I was so out of breath I could barely speak. 'Lil ... mara ... heading your way!'

'Mum?' she replied, anxiously. 'What's wrong?' I slowed down and tried to catch my breath, happy to let Andrew keep up the chase while I explained to Lily that the mara was hopping in the direction of the stables. I asked if she could run down to the lane and try to intercept it. She agreed, although I could tell she wasn't sure that she'd be able to do much to stop the animal who'd eluded capture for almost twenty-four hours. I wasn't sure my plan would work either, but it was the best option we had, so I hung up and picked up speed again, trying to catch up with Andrew who was hot on the heels of the speedy mara.

There was a hill leading up to the stables, and as Andrew and I started up the incline, both of us huffing and puffing now and dragging our nets behind us – I hadn't run so much since school! – we could see the tail of the mara bouncing over the crest of the hill. It was a real struggle to reach the top, I can tell you, but as we started the easier run down the slope, I caught sight of Lily standing in the middle of the road a few hundred yards ahead, holding a blanket from the stables like a matador's cape. Clever girl! She was using it to shoo the mara back in our direction and it seemed to be working. We both slowed down as we approached, gasping in enormous gulps of air and raising the nets to try and capture the mara once and for all. Lily looked up as we approached and in the split second that her attention was elsewhere, the mara tore off to the right, into a field. The three of us took off after it, not far behind this time. On fresher (and younger) legs than ours, Lily quickly took the lead and managed to overtake the animal, who was scampering along the edge of the field, sticking close to the hedgerow. Lily used her blanket to block its path, and as the mara turned to change direction, Andrew flung the net down. We had her! Quickly we transferred her into a carrying cage, put her in the back of the truck, and collapsed into the seats, exhausted.

When we got back to the park, and after a reviving cup of tea, we inspected the mara's enclosure. There was no way we were putting her back in there again until we knew it was completely secure. And as it was also Ringo's home, we needed to be doubly sure it was safe – the thought of him getting loose was terrifying! We'd have to issue an alert telling everyone to stay indoors. We scoured every inch of the fencing and could find no holes, and eventually we decided that the latch on the gate must have been nudged open by one of the alpacas in the enclosure next door. An unlikely partner-in-crime, but we could see no other obvious suspects. Andrew swiftly got out his toolbox and reinforced the latch, making sure there was no way the alpacas could aid any escapes ever again.

We've had a few other escapees over the years – not because the animals are unhappy in the park, but because they are wild animals at heart, and given the opportunity they will behave as such – but this was certainly the most dramatic!

RJ the raccoon was one of the first animals to move into Axe Valley Bird and Animal Park, and although I know we shouldn't have favourites, I must admit that he'll always have a special place in my heart. He's a solid, dependable sort of chap who rarely causes any mischief, and has always been popular with visitors at the park – I think it must be because he looks a bit like a cuddly teddy bear. Mind you, he might look cuddly and sweet, but RJ can be a bit of a grump. I think of him as an old man, set in his ways – if we could install an armchair and log fire in his pen, and provide him with a pipe and slippers, I think he'd be very happy. So when we decided recently that it was time to get him a mate, perhaps we should have known that he wouldn't cope well with the change. However, nothing ventured, nothing gained, as they say, and we introduced a female raccoon named CJ into his enclosure a few months ago. We've generally had a lot of success matchmaking pairs at the park – Mango and Tango, for example – so we really did hope that they'd hit it off straight away.

Although raccoons tend not to live in large social groups like meerkats, the experts say that they do prefer a bit of company and we even had hopes RJ and CJ might breed one day. A litter of baby raccoons would be brilliant. Unfortunately, for reasons best known to himself, RJ did not take to his suitor at all. To begin with she did her best to endear herself to him, but whenever she tried to be nice he just sat there in a huff, resolutely refusing to engage in any raccoon flirtation. In the end she gave up, and what's more, she took over his den and turfed him out of his own sleeping quarters! Poor old RJ – he seems to have come up against an alpha female, and I suspect he'll just have to give in to her will eventually. What's that they say about the female of the species?

He'll never admit it, but I suspect Andrew was secretly pleased to see RJ meet his match. You see, they had a run-in not that long ago, and I'm not sure all is forgiven just yet. After the positive response to the story about Wren and Rascal appeared in the local paper, they wanted to know more about what we were up to at Axe Valley and sent Richard back to the park to take some more pictures of our animals for a follow-up article. He wanted to get a shot of Andrew with RJ, and they set up a scene where Andrew was supposed to feed RJ one of his favourite treats – a hot cross bun. All was going well until RJ got a bit overexcited and mistook Andrew's finger for the bun! It was a nasty bite, and quickly put an end to that particular photo-shoot. We couldn't blame RJ for the injury, of course, but when Andrew walks past the raccoon enclosure and sees RJ being bossed around by his new lady friend, I'm not sure he feels *too* much sympathy.

Of course, we've all been on the receiving end of a few nips and scratches over the years – more often than not from my old pal Ringo. He's bitten Andrew on the back of the legs a few times and even on his lip before. He also had a go at Richard Austin when he dared to try and photograph him. His beak really is incredibly sharp and he'll easily draw blood if he manages to nip you. Now you understand why I go in to feed him wearing armour! I've also had a few scares over the years (I wouldn't want you to think I leave all the dangerous jobs to Andrew) including being charged by an angry tree porcupine. I'm sure I don't need to tell you how painful that could have been if she'd reached her target! Our porcupine, Jerry, had recently had a baby, and I was in her enclosure one day mucking out when I heard her come rattling down from the treehouse where she sleeps, faster than I'd ever seen her move before. I didn't immediately realise that she was coming for me – I must have overstepped the mark and moved too close to her baby – and just stood there, entranced. Porcupines are not known for their speed and it was incredible to see her moving at such a great rate. It was Lily, watching safely from the other side of the fence, who saw what was about to happen and shouted at me to run. I was about as far away from the gate to the enclosure as it was possible to be, and I had to leg it as fast as I could towards the fence and hurdle over it, praying as I did so that I had enough spring in my step to safely clear the three-foot barrier. I did, just. My landing on the other side wasn't particularly elegant, but I'd made it to safety in one piece. Jerry stood glaring at me from the other side, rattling her quills with menace. I certainly learnt my lesson that day, and from then on always exercised much more caution when entering her pen, or that of any mother who'd recently given birth.

Jerry's story is actually a very sad one. We've been very lucky with our animals over the years, and although of course we've lost a few to old age, we've – touch wood – had very few upsets otherwise. We had had a pair of tree porcupines – Jerry and her mate, Ben – for about four years, and I'd always hoped they might breed. But as the years went by, nothing ever seemed to happen, and they appeared to be content to live together side by side in their leafy enclosure. Then one day, completely out of the blue, Ben became ill. It's often difficult to detect changes in animals like the porcupines, who you can't handle and who are less vocal than some of their neighbours, but we noticed over the course of a few days that he wasn't emerging from the treehouse, and that there was food still left in their bowls at the end of the day. We called Tim, who prescribed some antibiotics and told us to keep a close eye on Ben. Sadly, the medicine didn't seem to help and one morning when I went to check on him, he had died during the night. We were all devastated – no one could understand what had happened, and it was the first time that one of our animals had deteriorated so quickly and unexpectedly. Lily and Jake were particularly upset, and we all shed a few tears that night.

After Ben's death we expected Jerry to pine for him, and sure enough she did become very listless, rarely coming down from the treehouse. I hoped that she hadn't caught the same illness, and watched her closely for any signs of real distress. Then, one day when I went to check on her, I found a tiny baby porcupine – a miniature little thing, covered in soft brown hair – in the undergrowth near to the ladder which led up to the treehouse. I couldn't believe it – that must have been why she'd been reluctant to leave her nest. It was a bittersweet moment: of course we were delighted, but it was so heartbreaking that Ben had died before the baby was born, particularly when we'd given up hope of them ever breeding. The fortunate thing about our job though is that there is little time to dwell on sadness – there's always something to do that will take your mind of it. The baby, named Solo, was so incredibly cute that we were soon all stopping by the porcupines' enclosure several times a day, hoping to catch a glimpse of the ball of fluff who had yet to grow her mother's thorny quills. It was around this time that I managed to accidentally provoke Jerry into her attack. Frightening as it was, I couldn't be cross with her – she was just protecting her baby from what she perceived to be a threat, something every mother understands. We continued to watch Solo develop from a safe distance, and consulted our books and the Internet to see when she would start to grow her spikes.

When Solo was about three months old, she suddenly and without any warning became very ill. Again we consulted Tim, who, despite all his best efforts, was at a loss to explain what might be wrong. The poor baby just lay there in the nest, not eating and breathing shallowly. It was just like what had happened to Ben, all over again. We kept a vigil at her side, and did everything we could to help her but all to no avail. Sadly, she died.

There are many moments of real happiness at Axe Valley. Every day something wonderful seems to happen: things which make us laugh out loud, or exclaim yet again how privileged we are to do what we do. We're privileged to witness some very special moments, and we never forget that. But every once in a while, tragedy strikes and reminds us all how cruel nature can be. It's a horrible lesson to learn, but one that is part and parcel of the work we do. And when these things happen, of course we shed a tear, and we never forget the animals we've lost, but then we must get up again the next day, and feed all the animals, and make sure those in our care are happy and well. And remind ourselves again how lucky we are.

Moving House

The journalist from the national newspaper called me early one morning, just as I was pulling on my wellies and preparing to head up to the park. I was still feeling anxious about appearing in such a big newspaper, but at least I knew what to expect from an interview this time. The journalist asked me many of the same questions as in the previous interview, and as I was very accustomed to telling Wren and Rascal's story by now, I chatted away happily for around half an hour. Her questions were a bit more in-depth, and she told me she planned to write the feature as if it was a diary, covering all the major events of the meerkats' first year. They would use some of Richard's pictures to illustrate it, and also wanted to see some of the snapshots we'd taken when Wren and Rascal were very small. She didn't know when the article would run, but she said her editor was very keen and we shouldn't have to wait too long.

After I'd said goodbye and hung up the phone, I stayed sitting in the kitchen for a few moments longer, looking over at the Aga where Wren and Rascal had spent those first precarious few hours. I couldn't believe so much had happened to us since then. We had celebrated their first birthday only a few weeks before, and they were now rambunctious young adults, nearly as big as Mango and Tango. We'd had a little family party in the kitchen, with plenty of Wren and Rascal's favourite food – mealworms – and a cake for us. They didn't know what all the fuss was about of course, but they're always delighted to be the centre of attention and certainly relished all the hugs and kisses they received that day. I was so pleased that they still seemed content to be a part of the family, and still allowed us to handle them. I had been told that they might start to become more independent after the first year and prefer to be left alone like the other meerkats at the park. I knew that if that happened, I'd have to let them be, but I couldn't imagine them not rushing over every time I walked by, or coming when I called their names.

When I finally tore myself away from the warm kitchen, I walked out into a world gilded by frost. It was a particularly cold February, and we'd had several days of extremely bitter weather. Everything looked so beautiful: the branches of the trees dusted with white, every blade of grass in the lawn crisp and glistening. I pulled my coat tightly around myself, and headed towards the park. It was all very well waxing lyrical about how pretty everything looked, but in this weather there was a lot of work to be done to make sure all the animals stayed warm. We had to make sure that everyone had enough bedding, extra protection from the elements, and that no one's water froze over. Animals that were particularly vulnerable were brought inside the barn at night, and Wren and Rascal were particularly pleased to be able to snuggle up to their old stuffed penguin in the toasty kitchen. They were my first port of call when I reached the park, and I was happy to see that they didn't seem to be too bothered by the cold. Quite the opposite in fact – they were rolling around in the bark, play-fighting with each other and apparently as happy as Larry. They paused their wrestling for a brief moment to receive a quick cuddle each, but soon resumed the rough and tumble. I've had visitors run up to me in alarm before, worried that Wren and Rascal were seriously fighting with each other. Their tussles can look quite aggressive, but they're really just playing and would never hurt each other.

I went over to one of the enclosures, where Andrew was repairing a bit of torn wire fencing. His fingers were so cold that it was a struggle to bend the wire the way he wanted it to go and he was muttering and cursing to himself. 'Cup of tea?' I asked. He looked like he could do with a break, and I was eager to tell him all about the interview. He nodded and hopped down from the ladder he'd been perched on, following me over to the kiosk. Once I'd made a brew, we swept the frost off one of the picnic benches and sat down, both wincing at the shock of the cold seats through our jeans.

'One day,' Andrew said, with that look he gets when he's hatching a grand plan, 'we should have a proper café here. If only so that we don't have to freeze our you-know-whats off every time we want a cuppa in winter.'

I smiled. This was a long-running campaign, and something we both hoped we'd be able to do – money and time permitting – in the not-too-distant future. 'Before we can even think about a café,' I replied, 'we need to seriously think about building a bigger enclosure for Wren and Rascal. They're getting too big for that one, and they need somewhere to shelter in the bad weather.'

Andrew nodded in agreement. 'It's just a case of getting the materials together,' he said. 'I know where it's going to go, but it'll need a fair amount of concrete and a couple of days' labour.'

He was right, but I was starting to worry about Wren and Rascal getting bored and frustrated in their current home as they continued to grow. There was nothing we could do about it for now though, so there was no point getting anxious.

'Go on then, tell me about this interview,' Andrew said. 'How long before you become a big celebrity and forget all about us?'

I laughed and told him how it had gone and that again we'd just have to wait and see when the article actually appeared. We were both hopeful that visitor numbers would get a real boost if we were featured in a national newspaper, although I was still strangely apprehensive about it all. I must have gone uncharacteristically quiet, because Andrew took my hand and reassured me that no one – no one we cared about, anyway – would think we were suddenly hungry for fame and fortune. Compared to a lot of the people you see in the newspapers and on reality TV these days, we were hardly selling our souls. It would just be a short feature, highlighting something we'd done that we hoped people would think was worthwhile. I knew he was right, but I couldn't help feeling worried about exposing everything we'd built to such scrutiny – what if people thought what we were doing was wrong? I knew there were people out there who didn't agree with keeping animals in captivity, and the last thing I wanted was to bring the park to their attention. We have had a couple of such people at the park in the past, and they waste no time in letting us know that they don't believe animals should ever be kept in cages. We've found there's no point in explaining that the animals we keep are all born and bred in captivity, and are an important educational resource. We both believe that the more people know about animals, their behaviour and their natural habitats, the more they will respect them – and that can only be a positive thing. But these people don't want to listen. They don't want to know that we're always trying to find ways to improve the conditions our animals live in – to build them bigger and better enclosures which more closely resemble their natural habitats. The animals we care for are content and healthy, and we really do love them all. I truly believe they are all happy at Axe Valley.

A few nights later, I was settling in for a cosy night in front of the TV, relieved to be warm for the first time that day. The temperature had dropped even further in the last twenty-four hours and it had been bitterly cold up at the park, in spite of the layers and layers of clothes I'd piled on. Jake and Lily were both upstairs

doing their homework and Andrew was off somewhere with his dad, so for once I had the TV all to
myself. I flicked through the channels looking for
something entertaining to watch, and clasped my fingers round my mug of tea, relishing the warmth. I
should have known better than to get too comfortable
though, for just as I'd settled on an episode of *Friends*,
Andrew came bursting into the lounge, waving my
coat.

'Great news! Adrian just called – he's got a load for
us. Come on, he'll be here in half an hour.'

My heart sank. Adrian is a friend of ours who
owns a concrete business and keeps his lorries
parked at the farm. He's helped us out in the past by
giving us the odd leftover bit of concrete from a load
when no one else needs it – many of our building
projects have got off the ground thanks to Adrian. In
many ways, this was perfect timing: we needed concrete to lay the groundwork for Wren and Rascal's
new enclosure. On the other hand, it was absolutely
freezing out there, and I was freshly showered and
warm and looking forward to a relaxing evening in
front of the fire. I looked at Andrew, I could tell he

was desperate to get going – his head already filled with plans. And I knew if I said I wasn't going to join him, he'd just go anyway and the job would take him twice as long. I sighed, cast one last longing glance at the TV, and grabbed my coat. It was going to be a long night.

Up at the park it was already dark, and we used our torches to guide us to the plot Andrew had already staked out for Wren and Rascal's new home. As I predicted, it was absolutely freezing, but I resolved to put on a brave face – for the time being, at least. My philosophy was the sooner we got this done, the sooner I could be back in front of the fire. By the time we'd reached the plot and made sure it was ready for the concrete, we could see the lights of Adrian's lorry approaching the farm gate. I walked down to meet him as he parked in his customary spot and Andrew went to warm up the tractor. We would have to move the concrete into the park using a relay system – tipping it first into the tractor's loader, then driving the tractor to the gates of the park before taking smaller loads up to the plot in wheelbarrows. It was unforgiving, repetitive work, trudging up and down the dark paths of the park with a barrow laden with heavy concrete. The muscles in my arms soon began to scream in protest and when I stumbled slightly on my fifth trip and banged my knee on the sharp edge of the barrow, I felt like bursting into tears. But I was determined to keep that brave face in place, and picked up the wheelbarrow once more, ploughing on. It must have taken at least an hour to get it all up there, but there was still more hard work to come. Once the load had been tipped onto the ground, Adrian said his goodbyes and Andrew and I were left with three tonnes of concrete to rake out smooth before we went to bed. It was already 9 p.m. and my fingers were numb from the cold, even with my thickest gloves. I could barely grip the rake, and found it hard to drag it through the thick, gloopy concrete – this was going to take hours. I kept up a running commentary of resentful mutterings in my head as I worked – cursing the meerkats for outgrowing their current home, cursing Adrian for his timing and cursing Andrew for being such a perfectionist. I knew he'd want to stay out here in the cold until the concrete was completely smooth and flat. Didn't the mafia use fresh concrete to dispose of bodies? Now there was an idea ...

Luckily for me (and him) Andrew might be a perfectionist, but he's also a quick worker and we actually finished the job in two hours, which wasn't bad going given the circumstances. As we trudged back to the house, muscles aching, Andrew sighed with satisfaction. 'That's a job well done,' he said. 'We can make a start on the rest of the enclosure tomorrow.' He grinned at me, noticing the look on my face. 'Don't worry, I'll get Dad to help me ... honestly, I thought you were going to push me in the concrete at one point up there.'

I smiled my sweetest smile. 'Me? Never crossed my mind.'

Wren and Rascal's grand new home was finished a week later, and what a sight it was. I had to admit when I saw the finished article that it was worth that one night of (extreme) discomfort. It was around nine times bigger than their previous home – a substantial upgrade – and had walls that were about four-foot high, with glass windows placed in them so that children could watch the meerkats playing without having to be lifted up by their parents. They had a luxurious sleeping compartment and a large mound in the centre of the enclosure made up of bark and various tree trunks so that they could burrow away to their hearts' content. The top of the mound is taller than the fence which surrounds the enclosure, so they can always see what's going on in the park and visitors are often welcomed by the sight of them adopting the classic meerkat pose: standing up proud and straight, their little front paws drawn up in front of them, alert to everything that's going on. I knew they'd be really happy there, and if they ever did reach an age where they no longer wanted cuddles and kisses from me, then I'd just have to be content knowing that they had this amazing home to live in.

The newspaper article ran a few days later. I couldn't believe it when I finally saw it – it was a whole page with an array of pictures (including that pesky one of me and the meerkats again) and mentioned the name of the park several times. It was also online, and I checked it regularly, eagerly reading the comments people had left. I was relieved to see they were all overwhelmingly positive, supporting us and saying nice things about Wren and Rascal. We even got comments from overseas, including a lovely one from America praising our 'wonderful story'. Perhaps this celebrity thing wouldn't be so bad after all?

Coming Full Circle

'Eighty-five, eighty-six, eighty-seven ... Eighty-seven!' Jake looked up from the notebook where he'd been totting up the day's visitor total, a grin on his face.

'Is that a record?' Mum asked, clearing dishes off the table. We'd just finished eating dinner sitting out on the decking with my parents. They'd both been roped into helping us out during the busy period at the park.

'Nope,' Jake shook his head. 'One day last week we had ninety-two and we're still trying to beat that. There are three weeks left of the summer holidays – we can totally do it!'

The big article had appeared in March, and since then we'd steadily been getting more and more visitors through the gates, but it was only when the schools broke up for summer that numbers started going through the roof. What was really weird was that people who lived only a few miles away but had never known about us before – despite our local advertising and the *Western Morning News* piece – suddenly started arriving in droves. When we asked them where they'd heard about the park they always, without fail, mentioned the newspaper article. 'You're the lady from the paper!' they'd say, before asking where they could see the meerkats. Everyone wanted to watch me handle them and, given how tame they still were, it was sometimes hard to explain why we couldn't allow Wren and Rascal to be held by anyone else. They are really good sports, but it isn't fair on them to be passed around from pillar to post and we can't be one hundred per cent sure that they won't take a nip at someone's finger if they start to get restless. It is much safer for them to be handled by people they know and trust.

By July, Wren and Rascal were nearly eighteen months old – as big as Mango and Tango and definitely adults. They had really settled into their new home and their role as the park's star attractions. I was amazed how many meerkat fans there seemed to be out there; people who'd been interested in them for years – I've lost track of the number of people who've told me that they'd loved the television programme *Meerkat Manor* or have travelled far and wide to see meerkats in various other zoos and wildlife parks. One elderly gentlemen arrived at the park accompanied by his carer – he told me that he'd cut the article out of the paper and had been carrying it around in his pocket for weeks until she was able to bring him to visit Wren and Rascal. I was so touched that he had made such an effort and it was fantastic to see him finally get to meet them.

We seemed to be averaging around eighty visitors every day, although Jake was keeping a close eye on the numbers and was determined to beat our existing record. It was exhausting but definitely worth all the hard work. Now that visitor numbers were so high there was a lot more general maintenance to be done and we liked to get all that out of the way before the first guests arrived – and that meant a lot of early starts.

It had been a blazingly hot day which had turned

into a perfect English summer's evening – it was still beautifully warm and everything in the garden was bathed in a soft golden light. I really cherish these moments when we can sit together and relax at last, reflecting on the day's events.

'Do you realise,' said Andrew, 'that we're now getting about *three times* as many visitors every day compared to when we started?'

'I remember those first few weeks,' said Dad. 'You were delighted just to get twenty-odd visitors in. Who would have thought that one day you'd be trying to beat ninety-two people?'

'Not me,' I replied, laughing. Of course we'd always been ambitious for the park, but these numbers were exceeding our wildest hopes. 'I think this calls for a toast, don't you?'

'Quite right,' agreed Andrew, raising his glass. 'Here's to Axe Valley Bird and Animal Park.'

'Cheers!' we all chimed in, clinking glasses.

'And to Wren and Rascal,' said Lily. 'I think they deserve a "cheers" of their own.'

She was right; none of this would have happened if it hadn't been for them. I raised my glass again.

'To Wren and Rascal. Thank you for putting Axe Valley on the map.'

'Wren and Rascal . . . Cheers!'

Two weeks later we were raising our glasses again. When Jake counted up the day's totals, he passed ninety-two and kept going, all the way to 104. A new record with only one week of the summer holidays to go. We'd actually done it.

As usual there was little time to reflect on our achievements, because grand plans were already underway. One of the benefits of our new-found popularity was that we now had the funds to make some of the improvements to the park that we'd long been dreaming of – starting with the café. This was to be the biggest building project we'd ever undertaken – a permanent structure which would provide visitors with an indoor area for their picnics and allow us to serve more hot drinks and snacks. We'd had to employ an architect to draw up the plans and then apply to the council for planning permission. It was a daunting process which reminded me of our

application to the Prince's Trust all those years ago –
the forms, the waiting, the feeling that all your hopes
and dreams are in the hands of someone you don't
know behind a faraway desk. It was only once everything had been officially approved and the visitor
numbers started to tail off after the holidays ended
that we'd be able to start work. They were due to let
us know any day now and we were all anxious about
it – Andrew was planning on doing most of the labour
himself and was chomping at the bit to make a start.
But like before, there was nothing to do but wait.

The next morning I did my usual eager check of the
post and email, hoping that word might finally have
arrived. There was nothing though, so with a sigh I set
off for the park; it was a Monday, the one day of the
week we're closed to the public, and I had a list of
things to do as long as my arm. I was relieved that it
was a bit cooler – the beautiful weather had been
great for bringing people out to the park, but with a
day of chores ahead it would be nice to have a bit of
respite from the sun. The first thing on my agenda
was to check in on our pair of coatis; coatis are related
to the raccoon, although they tend to be slightly

smaller and have longer, pointed snouts. The female was expecting a litter in the next week or so and we were keeping a close eye on her. It was her first pregnancy and she seemed quite nervous about the whole thing. But before I went to see them I couldn't resist a quick visit to say hello to Wren and Rascal and stopped off at the food shed to prepare them a snack – a mixture of dog biscuits and mealworms with a bit of fresh meat thrown in for good measure. They'd had such a busy day yesterday, with all 104 visitors spending at least five minutes at their enclosure. Somehow they seem to know when they're being watched and, natural performers that they are, always seem to put on a little show for their audience. They'd probably be exhausted today.

Wren was on sentry duty and I was chuffed to see that he didn't bark a warning to Rascal when he noticed my approach but instead ran down the mound to greet me. It could just have been that he'd spotted the food I was carrying, of course, but I like to think it was me he was excited to see. When I entered the enclosure they both ran over, writhing around my ankles with such enthusiasm that I nearly tripped.

'Hey!' I exclaimed. 'Steady on. You'll get your food in a minute.' I put the bowl down on the floor and perched on one of the logs in the enclosure, thinking that I'd just sit and watch them for five minutes before I went to check on the coatis. They both immediately climbed onto my lap, nudging at me with their little heads and chatting to each other in the way that I know means they're very happy. I couldn't help but smile – they might be all grown up now, and hungry and eager to tuck in to the food I'd brought, but they still weren't too old for a bit of love and affection. I gave each one a cuddle and then, satisfied, they both clambered down to attack the food. I watched them fighting over a bit of meat for a while – no playing nicely where food is concerned – and then headed over to the coatis' enclosure. We've had this pair since they were babies and I was really excited about the arrival of their first litter. In a few days' time we'd have to separate off the female before she gave birth, but for the time being she was still in the main enclosure with her mate. When I got there I noticed that he seemed agitated; he was pacing about and ignoring the fresh food in his bowl, which was very unusual. There was

no sign of the female and I was immediately concerned. We're always extra-cautious when one of our
animals is pregnant and because for some reason this
female had seemed to be very anxious about it, we'd
been particularly attentive. I shouted for Andrew to
come over, eager for his opinion. As I was waiting for
him to arrive, the female emerged from her mate's
sleeping box – she came out, waddled around in a
circle and then headed straight back inside again.
When Andrew arrived I told him what I'd seen and we
both stood there quietly to watch some more. The male
was still pacing about, and after about five minutes
the female emerged again from his box. This time she
walked nearer to us and we could see her more closely.
She seemed to be breathing very heavily. 'I think she's
already in labour,' said Andrew, confirming my sus-
picions. It was a worrying situation – now labour was
underway we wouldn't be able to separate her from
the male, which is what would have happened in the
wild. In an ideal world she would have been in an
enclosure on her own with a single sleeping compartment that she could nest in. We could only hope that
his presence wouldn't distress her too much.

Throughout the rest of the day we checked in regularly. It was difficult to see what was going on because she spent most of her time in her sleeping box but as far as we could tell, everything was going reasonably well and the male seemed to have settled down. We'd called Tim to let him know what was happening and he said there was nothing we could do but watch and be ready to step in when it was all over. I tried to get on with my chores but I found myself drawn back to their enclosure again and again – I was desperate to make sure nothing was wrong.

By early evening we thought it was probably safe to check on them so Andrew carefully entered the enclosure. He crouched down to check the female's sleeping compartment.

'There are three babies, Jayne!' he said. 'And they look nice and healthy. She looks fine too – they're all sleeping.' He looked relieved, but something was still niggling at me.

'Andrew, go and look in the other box,' I said. He looked puzzled and was about to say something, but I jumped in before he could object. 'Please. I just want to make sure everything's OK.' Still confused, but obviously realising I was serious, he walked the short distance to the male's sleeping compartment. Everything was quiet for a moment and I watched fretfully from the other side of the fence, hoping that my instincts were wrong. Andrew stood up, a grim look on his face.

'There are three more babies in there,' he said. 'They're not moving.'

I immediately hurried through the gate and squatted down next to the box. Peering inside I could just make out the three babies, huddled together in the straw. They were slightly bigger than Wren and Rascal had been but still completely bald and with their eyes shut. I reached in and tentatively touched the soft pink skin of the one nearest to me. It was cold but I could just feel the quivering of its tiny little heart. I reached in to cup them in my hand and pulled all of them out.

'We've got to get them inside,' I said, hurrying over to the gate. I can't explain what made me make Andrew check the other box; I just had a feeling that something wasn't right. It was unusual for a coati to have so many babies in a litter – they normally have only three or four – and she must have had these three first before moving into her own box to give birth to the remaining three. Although my mind was racing, I knew exactly what I needed to do. With Andrew right behind me I ran back to the house. I couldn't believe this was happening again ...

Afterword

Christmas, 2010

The coati babies went straight into the house and onto the Aga, which I knew would give them their best chance of survival. Sadly one baby died immediately and we lost another a few weeks later, but the third – named Zorro – is a hardy chap and is now living up at the park in his own enclosure. It was so strange to embark on this journey all over again – so much was the same and yet so much was different. I was more confident and sure of what I was doing, but coatis are very different animals to meerkats and in many ways Zorro was more of a challenge to hand-rear. He was incredibly active and an expert climber, so he was prone to get into more mischief right from the start. He would jump from my shoulder to Andrew's, or land on one of the children after launching himself off the top of a piece of furniture. Because he is an 'only child' he was far more dependent on us for entertainment and affection and all in all it was a much more exhausting process. He's a real character though, and we all love him to bits.

Zorro's mother raised all three of her other babies successfully and they have been re-homed with other zoos and wildlife parks. I'm sure that she would have been a brilliant mother to all six of her babies if circumstances had been different.

Wren and Rascal will be two years old in February. They're loving their five-star accommodation up at the park and are still very happy to be handled. I have noticed changes in them – they're obviously adults now and sometimes it's clear that they do just want to be left alone. I've become accustomed to picking up on their signals and if I sense that they're getting irritated or restless then we just give them some space and they're always back to their cheerful, friendly selves in no time at all.

At some point in the future we'll definitely intro-duce a female into their enclosure and see if they breed. As meerkat colonies only have one 'alpha' couple, Wren and Rascal will have to compete to win the affections of the female. I must admit that I'll be sorry to see the day when their close, brotherly bond is broken by the introduction of a female, but I know it's what would happen in the wild and it's a bridge that we'll just have to cross one day.

Planning permission for our café finally arrived and building work was finished by the end of the summer. Andrew worked really hard on it and we're both delighted that it's turned out so well. We have five tables, with seating for twenty, and a serving counter where visitors can buy hot and cold drinks, ice-creams, Mum's cakes and a variety of other snacks. Everyone pitches in to help out and all the visitors who saw the park before and after the café was built just can't believe the changes. It's all very rustic and cosy, with rough-hewn local timber used throughout, and decorated with homey bits and pieces.

Visitor numbers at the park are still really healthy, and we're looking forward to next summer when we hope we can beat the existing record.

When I look back over the past few years, I can't believe how much has happened. Our family life has continued as normal, just as it should have: Jake's had his football, Lily her horseriding, we've had a couple of short but much-needed holidays and a memorable trip up to London to see *The Lion King*. And the animals at Axe Valley have given us so much: yes, they've caused sleepless nights, they've sometimes even made us cry, but they've also made us laugh and have always given us love and affection. Even Ringo. But it is the two little meerkats who have really changed our lives. On that cold February morning in 2009, I had no idea what an impact they'd have. They've brought real joy to all of us, but also to the hundreds of people who've come to Axe Valley to visit them. We owe them a huge debt of thanks for the impact their arrival has had on the park – without them we never would have had 104 people through the gates in one day and certainly would never have been able to open the café, or at least not for a good few years. They have given us so much, but to be honest all that is secondary to the real truth. We love them and we couldn't be happier to have them as part of the family.

All about Axe Valley Bird and Animal Park

If you would like to meet Wren and Rascal or any of the other animals featured in *The Meerkats of Summer Farm* then why not pay a visit to Axe Valley Bird and Animal Park. We'd be delighted to see you!

Animals you can see at the park include:
RJ and CJ the lovelorn racoons
Ringo the bad-tempered crane
Max and Millie the very noisy otters
Zorro the amazing jumping coati
Meerkats Mango and Tango and all their family
Jerry the tree porcupine

Ruby and Clancy the wallabies, the longest-serving residents of Axe Valley

Echo the owl

Our incredible escaping mara

... and lemurs, skunks, deer, kune kune pigs, chipmunks, pygmy goats, chinchillas, peacocks, barn owls, tawny owls, rabbits, guinea pigs, chickens, parrots, kookaburras and heron.

And, of course, Amber, Willow, Tarka, Blue, Wren and Rascal.

The park is open every day except Monday from 10 a.m. to 5 p.m., including bank holidays and school holidays. You can find us on the B3261 (just off the A35) between Axminster and Honiton – just follow the signs!

For more information please go to our website www.axevalleypark.co.uk

Hope to see you soon!

Jayne, Andrew, Lily and Jake

Acknowledgements

First and foremost, we'd like to thank both our parents – Alan and Val and Mike and Jill – whose love and support has given us the confidence to get our idea off the ground. And Duncan, Sally, Guy and Zara; Nick, Ali, Seth and Charlotte; Trudy, Erik, Katie, Ella and Lotta and Emma and Scott who are always around to help when asked ... which is quite often!

Barbara Nash who fitted in to our family with ease

Hannah Boursnell – thank you for all your help and guidance

Adrian and Emma Clarke – nothing is too much trouble; always happy to help us at the drop of a hat

Tom and James Clarke – our most willing and able concrete shifters

Mark Jones – a true friend. Always willing to help us come rain or shine

Richard Bevis – a generous and thoughtful friend

Richard Austin – great photos that started the ball rolling

Tim Lawrence – available 24/7 for veterinary advice

Mervyn and Kate Anstey – fantastic, supportive friends

Richard Saxby

Bob Barathy

Daniel Cullen

Danny and Lyn Reynolds

Derek and Sarah Gibson